Jean Colbert Dias

The relationship between the stabilisation of interim relief and res judicata

Jean Colbert Dias

The relationship between the stabilisation of interim relief and res judicata

Similarities and dissimilarities

ScienciaScripts

Imprint
Any brand names and product names mentioned in this book are subject to trademark, brand or patent protection and are trademarks or registered trademarks of their respective holders. The use of brand names, product names, common names, trade names, product descriptions etc. even without a particular marking in this work is in no way to be construed to mean that such names may be regarded as unrestricted in respect of trademark and brand protection legislation and could thus be used by anyone.

Cover image: www.ingimage.com

This book is a translation from the original published under ISBN 978-613-9-66963-9.

Publisher:
Sciencia Scripts
is a trademark of
Dodo Books Indian Ocean Ltd. and OmniScriptum S.R.L publishing group

120 High Road, East Finchley, London, N2 9ED, United Kingdom
Str. Armeneasca 28/1, office 1, Chisinau MD-2012, Republic of Moldova, Europe
Printed at: see last page
ISBN: 978-620-7-69364-1

"I dedicate this work to my family, with special affection for my wife Elaine and my children Joao Vitor and Elisa, without forgetting my parents Colbert and Rosilda who bless me from heaven."

"The legal profession is not a profession for cowards."

Sobral Pinto

SUMMARY

This book looks at the new Civil Procedure Code that came into force in 2015, paying special attention to the chapter that deals with interim relief. It also conceptualizes res judicata under the new procedural optics in comparison with the phenomenon of stabilization of interim relief. The main objective of the work is to show the superficial similarities between res judicata and the stabilization of interim relief, which, in a less accurate analysis, can generate slight conceptual confusions and can even raise questions about the constitutionality of the technique of stabilizing interim relief, which comes from a summary judgment, but which, with the passage of time, can gain immutability and indisputability, just like res judicata. It will also demonstrate the dissimilarities between res judicata and the stabilization of interim relief, which sharply diverge when analyzed in the context of their formation. In this comparison, it will be shown that res judicata, despite a certain appearance of correlation with the stabilization of interim relief, actually has no conceptual relationship with the latter, since it is obtained through an exhaustive judgment. A study will be devoted to the adoption of the technique of stabilizing preliminary injunctions as a means of making judicial protection more effective, especially by mitigating the harmful effects of time on the process and the parties' claims.

Keywords: Interim relief. Stabilization of preliminary injunctions. Res judicata. Similarities and dissimilarities.

SUMMARY

INTRODUCTION

The aim of this book is to clearly identify the two procedural institutes (res judicata and stabilization of interim relief), conceptualizing and presenting their characteristics and primary purposes in order to, at first, rule out any possibility of confusion between them and, at a second stage, demonstrate that technically they are very different, but that some of their effects appear to be similar.

The first chapter deals specifically with res judicata and its main characteristics, notably demonstrating its legal effects and its practical effects to the detriment of interim relief and the phenomenon of stabilization.

At the start of the study, we sought to establish the limits of res judicata and its control mechanisms, a subject which has generated some controversy in the legal community, with some authors arguing for the broadest possible way of overturning res judicata. On the other hand, the prevailing doctrine has set its sights on the immutability of res judicata, relegating the possibility of its revision to very few situations, whose position is based on the constitutional principle of legal certainty.

The second chapter highlights the crucial difference between definitive and provisional relief, and also differentiates between satisfactory provisional relief and precautionary provisional relief.

Another important point is the presentation of injunctive relief in terms of when it can be sought, i.e. as an incidental measure or in advance, making it clear that it is only in the second case that the phenomenon of stabilization materializes.

The second part of the work also deals with the differences between precautionary injunctions and satisfactory injunctions, especially when they are granted in advance. These situations have been given their own chapters in the new Civil Procedure Code, but only satisfactory injunctions can be affected by the phenomenon of stabilization.

The necessary explanation of evidentiary relief to the detriment of urgent relief could not be left out, specifically pointing out its requirements and making it clear that the first hypothesis does not require the characterization of the requirement of danger of delay or the possibility of damage, but rather the clarity of the right invoked and the probability of success at the end of the demand.

The third chapter deals with the stabilization of the satisfactory injunctive relief, bringing up the assumptions for its granting and its special characteristics, since this procedural institute is an innovation of the Civil Procedure Code that came into force in 2015, despite the fact that a similar institute is already known in Brazilian law through the monitoring action procedure, which was maintained in the current Code.

In the final chapter, there is a very clear concern on the part of academics about the plaintiff's procedural loyalty with regard to the continuation of the main action in the event of the satisfactory provisional injunction being granted in advance (stabilized), making it clear that the plaintiff must make his intention clear beforehand so as not to cause damage or surprise the defendant, who may be satisfied with the stabilization of the decision and wish to alleviate his procedural problems.

In addition, concern is expressed about the questioning of some scholars regarding the stabilization of the satisfactory provisional protection granted in advance, mainly due to the fact that stabilization occurs after a summary judgment, a situation that is markedly different from res judicata, which is obtained through an exhaustive judgment.

On the other hand, this work has also sought to establish parameters for the best way to challenge a decision that tends to stabilize, following the path indicated by the legislator, but not failing to find options to avoid stabilization by other means of procedural insurgency on the part of the defendant, also dealing with the action for challenge and its statute of limitations.

The constitutionality of the phenomenon of stabilization has been widely debated, with some scholars arguing that it is constitutionally inadequate in view of the effects of stabilization and the impossibility of generating some of the practical effects of res judicata.

Despite the alleged dissimilarities between res judicata and the stabilization of interim relief, after much debate we can't agree that the effects of both are close from a practical point of view, even if conceptually they are very far apart, however, there is no denying that they culminate in unassailable decisions, in other words: "immutable" and "indisputable".[1]

Furthermore, the new procedural model of stabilizing provisional injunctions should be seen as an attempt to speed up the delivery of judicial services, since the unjustified delay in effective judicial protection caused by the slowness of the Judiciary, which is actually the denial of justice itself.[2]

This is why we will see in this book the clear differentiation between res judicata and the stabilization of provisional injunctions. However, we cannot deny that certain practical effects - although disassociated from a conceptual point of view - are similar, and that if they are well used by legal operators and correctly delimited by the Judiciary when they are applied, they tend to provide agility and less painful solutions for litigants in court cases.

[1] MARINONI, Luiz Guilherme; ARENHART, Sergio Cruz; MITIDIERO, Daniel. **Civil Procedure Course**. Sao Paulo: RT, 2015, vol. 2, p. 216.
[2]THEODORO JR., Humberto. **Anticipated Injunction - Evolution - Comparative View - Brazilian Law and European Law**. Scientific bases for a renewed procedural law. Sao Paulo: Instituto Brasileiro de Direito Processual Brasileiro vol.1, mai.- 2008, p. 424.

1 JUDGMENT

1.1 CONCEPT

It is immediately crucial to discuss res judicata at the beginning of this study and then work on the subject of interim relief in consonance with res judicata in order to finally develop the main subject of the similarities or dissimilarities between the stabilization of interim relief and res judicata.

With regard to the concept of res judicata, the legislator intended to define its guidelines in article 502 of the new CPC: "Res judicata is the authority that renders a decision on the merits immutable and indisputable and no longer subject to appeal".

The doctrine interprets the above-mentioned procedural provision from two perspectives: firstly, res judicata as an "authority" and secondly, the effects of this "authority" from the point of view of the indisputability and immutability of the decision:

> Firstly, it considers res judicata to be an "authority". "Authority" is a legal situation: the force that qualifies a decision as binding and definitive. As a legal situation, res judicata is a legal effect - an effect that arises from a given legal fact, after the incidence of the legal norm. In the second part, art. 502 of the CPC lays down the two corollaries of this authority: the decision becomes indisputable and immutable.[3]

In this sense, it can be said that indisputability can be seen in two dimensions: in the first, res judicata prohibits/prevents the same issue from being the subject of a new decision, which doctrine has called the negative effect of res judicata; in the second, res judicata must be observed when it forms the basis of a claim, which is called the positive effect of res judicata.

The positive effect of res judicata in the first court decision is binding on other judges who come to deal with the issue later.

---

[3] DIDIER JR, Fredie; BRAGA, Paula Sarno; OLIVEIRA, Rafael Alexandria de. **Civil Procedure Course**. 10 ed., Bahia: Editora Jus PODIVM, 2015, v. 2, p. 513.

Therefore, even from the point of view of indisputability, res judicata generates an acquired right for the court, which cannot be attacked by another court decision.

> The negative effect of res *judicata* operates as an *exceptio rei iudicatae,* i.e. as a defense, to prevent a new trial of what has already been decided in the previous case. The positive effect, on the other hand, corresponds to the use of res judicata itself in its content, making it imperative for the second trial. While the *exceptio rei iudicatae* is a form of defense, to be used by the defendant, the positive effect of res judicata can be the basis of a second claim.[4]

Lastly, res judicata is also immutable and cannot be altered, but, although this is the rule, there are situations in which a decision that has passed through res judicata and gained the *status of res judicata* can be reviewed or undone, as will be discussed below.

1.2 THE LEGAL EFFECT OF RES JUDICATA AND ITS PRESUPPOSITIONS

As Eduardo Talamini says: "Res judicata is a legal effect that derives from the law, which takes the decision as just one of its presuppositions"[5] , in other words, the decision is not the legal fact of res judicata, in fact the decision makes up the legal fact of res judicata.

There is a great deal of debate in Portuguese doctrine as to whether res judicata is an effect of the decision or not, and there are three respectable positions:

There is debate about what constitutes res judicata: a) the declaratory element of the decision (a German concept developed by Hellwig, Rosenberg etc. and adopted in Brazil by Pontes de Miranda, Ovidio Baptista da Silva, Araken de Assis etc.); b) the effects of the decision, not just the declaratory element, as argued by Liebman; c) the content of the decision, as argued by Jose Carlos Barbosa Moreira.); b) on the effects of the decision, as Liebman

[4] SILVA, Ovidio Baptista da. **Civil Procedure Course. Process of Knowledge**. 5 ed. Sao Paulo: RT, 2000, v. 1, p. 500.
[5] TALAMINI, Eduardo. Res **judicata and its revision**. Sao Paulo: RT, 2005, p. 45.

argues; c) on the content of the decision, not just the declaratory one, as Jose Carlos Barbosa Moreira argues. In fact, there is a famous polemic on the subject between Barbosa Moreira and Ovidio Baptista da Silva, with several texts produced by them.[6]

What is certain in articles 502 and 503 of the CPC is that res judicata establishes the indisputable and immutable nature of the decision, regardless of which position is taken, whether it recognizes that the effects are present in the declaration or that they are in the constitution or condemnation of the *decision.*

In this vein, since res judicata is a legal effect that derives from a legal fact, considered as a composite, we can conclude that res judicata is the result of the combination of two facts[7] : a) a court decision based on exhaustive cognition; b) res judicata.

With regard to "item a", although art. 502 of the CPC states that a decision on the merits is a prerequisite for res judicata, there are situations in which this premise does not hold true, and the new CPC embraces the possibility of an interlocutory decision becoming indisputable and immutable through the stabilizing process of res judicata, but rooted in a summary cognition judge, whose phenomenon has been baptized as the stabilization of provisional relief.

With regard to "item b", it is required that the court decision can no longer be attacked by any ordinary (total) or extraordinary (partial) appeal, i.e. that it cannot be challenged by any suitable appeal, except as already established by case law in the case of untimely filing of an appeal, the filing of motions for clarification repeatedly (three times), etc.

Finally, it should not be forgotten that res judicata, when invoked, gives more life to the constitutional principle of legal certainty, when it gives solidity to acquired rights, including protecting res judicata from any subsequent

---

[6] DIDIER JR, Fredie; BRAGA, Paula Sarno; OLIVEIRA, Rafael Alexandria de. **Civil Procedure Course**. 10 ed., Bahia: Editora Jus PODIVM, 2015, v. 2, p. 515.
[7] DIDIER; BRAGA e OLIVEIRA, *op. cit.,* p. 516.

legislation (art. 5, XXXVI, CF/88).

1.3 FORMAL AND MATERIAL RES JUDICATA

Although art. 502 of the CPC is limited to the definition of res judicata, formal res judicata is visible to the naked eye, as it is implicit in art. 505 of the same law, which states: "No judge shall decide again matters already decided relating to the same dispute,...", i.e. it prevents the judge from re-examining, within the same process, matters already decided or even precluded.

Humberto Theodoro Jr. differentiates the two types of res judicata very well:

> In fact, the difference between res judicata and formal res judicata is only one degree of the same phenomenon. Both stem from the impossibility of appealing against the judgment. Formal res judicata simply results from the immutability of the judgment within the proceedings in which it was handed down due to the impossibility of appeals, either because the law no longer allows them, or because the time limit stipulated by the law has expired without an appeal by the loser, or because the appellant has given up the appeal or waived it.[8]

If the decision is unchangeable, the process "exhausts the jurisdictional function". The State, through its judicial body, "delivers the judicial service to which it was obliged". But immutability, which prevents the judge from making a new judgment in the process, also has repercussions for the parties outside the process, preventing them from renewing the dispute in other processes. For litigants subject to *res iudicata,* the command emerging from the judgment is projected "also outside the proceedings in which it was handed down, due to the immutability of its effects".

In short, formal res judicata occurs and generates its effects within the proceedings in which the judgment was handed down, without preventing the matter from being assessed in a new judgment in a future or concurrent

[8] THEODORO JR., Humberto. **Civil Procedure Course.** 56 ed. Rio de Janeiro: Forense, 2015, vol. 1, p. 1598-1599.

proceeding, as can be seen from art. 486 of the CPC[9] , while material res judicata, because it has the force of law between the parties, produces effects not only within the proceedings but in any other.

In the same vein, the aforementioned author states:

> Formal res judicata can exist on its own in a given case, as is the case with merely final judgments, which only extinguish the proceedings without judging the case. But material res judicata can only occur in conjunction with formal res judicata, i.e. every judgment must also be formally res judicata if it is to become res judicata materially.[10]

Already flirting with the main object of the study, some scholars believe that the list of decisions that do not involve the resolution of the dispute, and therefore would not be covered by res judicata, would include: *(i)* expedient orders and interlocutory decisions on matters not related to the merits; *(ii)* sentences handed down in voluntary jurisdiction procedures; *(iii)* provisional decisions handed down in the field of urgent or evidentiary relief, which can be revoked or modified at any time (art. 296 of the Civil Code). 296), in an allusion to § 6 of art. 304, which provides for the possibility of stabilizing the measure that provisionally anticipates the effects of the resolution of the merits of the case.

1.4 LIMITS OF RES JUDICATA

Res judicata exerts its force in four very clear areas: territorial (geographical location), temporal (length of time), subjective (for which people) and objective (on which issues).

The basic criterion for identifying res judicata is called *triple identity,* where the first limits of res judicata are established, i.e. there is res judicata when an action that has already been judged by a final and unappealable

---

[9] Art. 486. A court ruling that does not resolve the merits does not prevent the party from bringing the action again.
[10] THEODORO Jr., Humberto. **Civil Procedure Course**. 56 ed. Rio de Janeiro: Forense, 2015, vol. 1, p. 1598-1599.

judgment is repeated in court, as stated in art. 337, § 4, of the CPC[11] .

In other words, traditionally the criterion of *triple identity* is seen in the hypothesis that one action is identical to another when they have the same parties, the same cause of action and the same claim (art. 337, § 2), the requirements of which, used in line with art. 502 of the CPC, serve as a beacon for identifying res judicata, but other more complex limits are used for this purpose.

1.4.1 Territorial boundaries

From an individual point of view and from the point of view of its territorial limitation, res judicata is binding and generates practical effects according to the extent of the jurisdiction recognized by law for the decision-maker, be it a single judge or a court, and it is also necessary to distinguish the origin of the res judicata, whether it came from a national, foreign or international court.

As stated in article 16 of the CPC, "Civil jurisdiction shall be exercised by the judges and courts throughout the national territory, in accordance with the provisions of this Code", the decisions handed down by a local judge shall have force throughout the national territory, however, the obvious issues of jurisdiction and competence that do not require further elucidation should be highlighted here.

With regard to judgments handed down by a foreign court, res judicata will only operate on national territory once it has been internalized by the homologation of the foreign judgment before the Superior Court of Justice (art. 960 et seq. of the CPC).

---

[11] Art. 337. Before arguing the merits, the defendant must allege:
[...]
§ Paragraph 2. An action is identical to another when it has the same parties, the same cause of action and the same claim.
[...]
§ Paragraph 4. Res judicata exists when an action that has already been decided by a final and unappealable decision is repeated.

Unlike foreign res judicata, international res judicata comes from international courts, whose jurisdiction derives from whether or not a country has signed up to international treaties and conventions, and therefore, unlike the former, does not require homologation in order to take effect on national territory.

1.4.2 Time limits

It can be said that as long as the elements of fact and law that characterized the case and gave rise to the dispute remain unscathed, res judicata maintains its effects and binds the parties or interested third parties as to its decisional content.

The doctrine states that:

> Thus, the temporal limits of res judicata indicate "from when" and "until when" res judicata exerts its influence. Normally, the temporal binding of res judicata is dealt with by applying the maxim - originating from Roman contract law - "*contractus qui habent tractum successivum et dependentiam defuturo, rebus sic stantibus intelliguntur*", invoked as a rule in its abbreviated form, *"rebus sic stantibus": res* judicata binds as long as the state of things remains the same.[12]

It is precisely for this reason that article 505 of the CPC establishes that *"no judge shall decide again matters already decided concerning the same dispute",* except *"if, in the case of a continuing legal relationship, there has been a change in the state of fact or law", at* which time the interested party may bring a new action seeking a review of what was decided in the judgment, a situation which is repeated in the other cases provided for by law.

This does not mean that the judge will decide the "same case", because the change in the state of fact or law gives rise to a new case, which has not yet been submitted to the scrutiny of the Judiciary, however, it must not be forgotten that the new judicial decision cannot revert to a previous

[14] MARINONI, Luiz Guilherme; ARENHART, Sergio Cruz; MITIDIERO, Daniel. **Course on Civil Procedure**. Sao Paulo: RT, 2015, vol. 2, p. 630-631.

situation and obviously does not retroact its effects.

1.4.3 Subjective limits

As res judicata has the effect of law in the specific case, these effects and their limits, which go beyond the interests of the parties, will have to be analyzed, not least because there are situations in which third parties are affected by the judicial decision without having a specific procedural interest, and with this in mind the doctrine deals with the subjective limits of res judicata.

The current CPC deals with the subject in article 506: "A judgment is res judicata for the parties between whom it is given, without prejudice to third parties". As a general rule, only the parties are covered by res judicata, since they participated in the adversarial process and used the means to defend their rights in the process that resulted in the court decision which, in the end, became indisputable and immutable.

> Naturally, if these parties were able to influence the delivery of the judicial decision, they must undoubtedly be subject to the judicial response offered. Also subject to res judicata are the procedural substitute (art. 18), the successor by universal title and the successor to the thing in dispute (art. 108 and 109), with the exception, of course, of the good faith of the third party purchaser. In these cases, the *legal link* with the parties authorizes the binding of res judicata. For the parties and their successors, therefore, the court decision, which is preclusive due to the exhaustion of the means of challenging it, becomes immutable.[13]

But there remains a doubt in the air about third parties who have not been involved in the procedural dispute, but who have felt the intermediate or immediate effects of the resolution of the dispute. The current CPC has not reproduced the old 472, sole paragraph of the repealed Code, according to which "in cases relating to the status of a person, if all the interested parties have been summoned to the proceedings in necessary litigation, the judgment

[14] MARINONI, Luiz Guilherme; ARENHART, Sergio Cruz; MITIDIERO, Daniel. **Course on Civil Procedure**. Sao Paulo: RT, 2015, vol. 2, p. 630-631.

shall produce res judicata in relation to third parties".

Thus, the new Code does not prevent third parties from benefiting from res judicata, in other words, it allows res judicata to be formed *secundum tenorem rationis,* in harmony with Article 274 of the Civil Code, according to which the third party, creditor or joint debtor, provided that the outcome of the proceedings was favorable to them and not based on a special quality linked solely to the plaintiff or defendant, can take advantage of res judicata formed *inter alias.*

> A court judgment can have *effects on* all these subjects, whether they are parties, interested third parties or even indifferent third parties. These effects, however, will be felt and received differently depending on the condition of the subject who suffers them. To translate this idea into an example: a judgment that orders someone's eviction will undoubtedly have effects on the tenant (who will have to leave the property), but also on his family (who will accompany him), his friends (who will recognize that he no longer lives there), his creditors (who, in order to collect disputed debts, will have to look for him at his new address) and so on. In the same way, the judgment will apply to the subtenant who has rented a room in the rented property.
>
> All these people, whether or not they took part in the process that resulted in the eviction, suffer the effects of the court decision to a greater or lesser extent. But is there a difference between the quality of the effects they suffer? Undoubtedly, yes. Those who have an interest that qualifies as *legal in* relation to the litigation and the outcome can - *because they have legal standing to do so* - oppose, in some way, their legal sphere being affected by these effects.[14]

In short, it is clear that those who are not parties to the case cannot be affected by the effects of res judicata, they can only be affected in a positive or negative way by the effects of the judgment, so they can oppose the case as third parties or even discuss the effects of the judgment later in a new lawsuit, as they are not directly affected by res judicata.

[14] MARINONI, Luiz Guilherme; ARENHART, Sergio Cruz; MITIDIERO, Daniel. **Course on Civil Procedure**. Sao Paulo: RT, 2015, vol. 2, p. 630-631.

1.4.4 Objective limits

The objective limitation of res judicata aims precisely to establish what this institute covers and which issues can no longer be debated by the parties. This can be materialized through the *objective limits of res judicata* (arts. 503 and 504) and partly through the *preclusive effect of res judicata* (art. 508).

> The answer seems to be quite simple, not least because of the definition adopted here. If this phenomenon affects the declaration contained in the judgment and if this declaration can only exist with the judicial response to the claim, it is certain that res judicata will only affect the operative part of the judgment. As art. 504 states, "reasons, even if important for determining the scope of the operative part of the judgment", and the "truth of the facts, established as the basis of the judgment", do not become res judicata. Thus, the issues of the case expressly decided by the operative part of the judgment acquire the immutability characteristic of res judicata (art. 503, caput).[15]

It remains to be analyzed what may or may not be the subject of the operative part of a court judgment, on the first level obviously the facts and allegations brought by the parties to the proceedings as a form of action, defense and even counterclaim will be covered by res judicata (art. 503, caput). 503, *caput*), on a second level the preliminary issues duly alleged by the parties or even independently of the request if it is necessary for the judge to analyze them in order to give effect to the main request, may form the operative part of the judgment (art. 503, § 1), except when there are evidentiary restrictions or limitations on cognition that prevent further analysis of the preliminary issue (art. 503, § 2).

> A prejudicial issue is one that conditions the content of the judgment on another issue, which in this perspective is seen as a subordinate issue. Thus, the mere precedence of one issue in relation to another is not enough to characterize prejudiciality.[16] In a maintenance action, for example, the relationship of kinship (natural or socio-affective) between the plaintiff and the defendant is a prejudicial issue to the consideration of the right to maintenance. Another example: in an action for rent, the existence of a rental agreement is prejudicial to the right to an order. In such cases, the

---

[15] MARINONI, Luiz Guilherme; ARENHART, Sergio Cruz; MITIDIERO, Daniel. **Civil Procedure Course**. Sao Paulo: RT, 2015, vol. 2, p. 632.
[16] MENESTRINA, Francesco. **La pregiudiciale nel processo civil.** p. 97, *apud* MARINONI; ARENHART e MITIDIERO, 2015, p. 632.

> resolution of the first issue (the relationship of kinship, the existence of a lease) conditions the content of the judgment on the second issue (the right to maintenance, the right to rent): if the judge decides that there is no kinship or no lease, logically there is no right to maintenance and no right to rent. However, if the judge finds that there is a relationship or a tenancy, then he or she must consider other issues (for example, the necessity-possibility binomial for maintenance, the existence of default for rent) in order to judge the right to maintenance and the right to rent.
> In order to be the subject of the provision, however, it is not enough for it to be a preliminary issue. The new Code expressly states that the preliminary issue that can be decided with the force of res judicata is only that on which the "judgment on the merits depends." (art. 503, § 1, I). That is to say: as the doctrine states,[17] only the preliminary question that constitutes a *necessary basis for* the resolution of the preliminary question can achieve the authority of res judicata.[18]

Ultimately, the limits to res judicata lie in the issues expressly decided by the judgment in the operative part, either at the instigation of the parties or at the initiative of the judge, where the legislation authorizes him to act in this way, otherwise all other issues that are outside the operative part, but within the grounds, are excluded from the possibility of res judicata.

1.5 PRECLUSIVE EFFECT OF RES JUDICATA

The preclusive effect of res judicata is enshrined in article 508 of the CPC: "Once the decision on the merits has become final, all allegations and defenses that the party could oppose either to the acceptance or rejection of the claim shall be deemed to have been presented and rejected", in other words, all the arguments and evidence that the parties could allege or produce in defense of their thesis, whether coming from the plaintiff or the defendant, become irrelevant.

> With the formation of res judicata, the possibility of re-discussing all the arguments - "allegations and defenses", in the legal definition - that could have been raised, but were not, ceases. *Res judicata forecloses* the possibility of discussing what was deduced and makes it irrelevant to raise what could have been deduced (the deducible); *res* judicata covers the res *deducta* and the *res deducenda.*
> [...]

---

[17] LOPES, Bruno. **Limites objetivos e eficacia preclusiva da coisa julgada,** p. 81, *apud* MARINONI; ARENHART e MITIDIERO, 2015, p. 632.
[18] MARINONI; ARENHART and MITIDIERO, *op. cit.,* 2015, p. 633-634.

> Not even issues that should be analyzed at any time, such as the lack of procedural requirements, can be raised - "at any time" should be understood as "at any time until res judicata".
> [...]
> The obvious exceptions here are material errors and calculation errors, since the decision that contains them does not become final (art. 494, CPC). This is also true of the cases in which a final decision can be rescinded (art. 966, CPC), which show vices and injustices capable of surviving even the preclusive effect of res judicata.[19]

The Superior Court of Justice has ruled along these lines:

> SPECIAL APPEAL. CIVIL AND CIVIL PROCEDURE. STATUTE OF LIMITATIONS ON CLAIMS FOR DAMAGES. PLEA IN THE JUDGMENT ENFORCEMENT PHASE. INVALUABLE.
> 1. There is a statute of limitations on the claim for compensation brought after the final and unappealable judgment granting the claim has been passed in the enforcement phase.
> 2. Once a final and unappealable judgment has been handed down in an action for damages, the preclusive effect of res judicata arises, preventing even matters of public policy, such as the statute of limitations on the claim for damages, from being dealt with in the enforcement phase.
> 3. SPECIAL APPEAL DISMISSED.[20]

On the other hand, it is not at all easy to ascertain in a specific case which of the plaintiff's allegations could be deemed to have been rejected by the final and unappealable decision: "do the allegations have to be related to the same cause of action, in other words new arguments on the same grounds? Or is there an implicit judgment on a *cause of action* not raised?".[21]

There are three currents of thought on the subject, the majority of which believe that the preclusive effect only affects the arguments and evidence that were used to support the cause of action brought by the plaintiff. In this line of reasoning, there are renowned scholars who claim that the preclusive effect does not affect all causes of action, but only the *cause petendi* that underpinned the claim formulated by the plaintiff and obviously the allegations that refer to it. They therefore believe that it is possible to bring a new action with the same claim, as long as it is based on a new cause of

[19] DIDIER JR, Fredie; BRAGA, Paula Sarno; OLIVEIRA, Rafael Alexandria de. **Civil Procedure Course**. 10 ed., Bahia: Editora Jus PODIVM, 2015, v. 2, p. 547.
[20] STJ , 3ª Turma, REsp n. 1.381.654, rel. min. Paulo de Tarso Sanseverino, j. 05.11.2013, published in the Dje of 11.11.2013. In the same vein: STJ , 2ª Turma, AgRg no RMS 4042 2/RO, rel. Min. Castro Meira, j. em 11.06.201 3, publicado no Dje de 18.06.2013.
[21] TESHEINER, Jose Maria. **Efficacy of sentences and res judicata in civil proceedings**. Sao Paulo: RT, 2001, p. 156.

action.[22]

On the other hand, another respectable group of scholars maintain that the preclusive effect of res judicata covers all possible causes of action that could have been the basis of the claim. For them, res judicata encompasses all the causes of action that could have been alleged, but in practice were not.[23]

Finally, the third current, headed by Jose Maria Tesheiner, believes that the preclusive effect of res judicata reaches all legal facts of the same nature, of the same essence, which could serve to support the claim made, even if they consist of different causes of action. The author argues that the important thing is to identify whether the facts narrated are substantially similar.

To support his thesis, he gives an example:

> [...] if the plaintiff files for eviction, alleging damage to the walls of the property, he cannot file another claim alleging damage to the doors, unless it occurred after the instruction was closed. However, he is not prohibited from filing, concurrently or subsequently, an eviction suit based on a non-consensual tenancy, because this is a fact of a different nature".[24]

Analyzing the three currents, the majority position seems to be the most authoritative, since it allows a new claim to be brought, provided that one of its identifying elements (cause of action) is modified, returning to the Judiciary the assessment of the right with the aim of providing a judicial service.

---

[22] MOREIRA, Jose Carlos Barbosa. **Preclusive efficacy of res judicata in the Brazilian civil procedure system**. Themes of Procedural Law. Sao Paulo: Saraiva, 1977, p. 99 and 103-108; ARAGAO, Egas Dirceu. **Sentence and res judicata**. Rio de Janeiro: AIDE, 1992, p. 324325; MITIDIERO, Daniel. Res judicata**, objective limits and preclusive efficacy**. Introduction to the Study of Civil Procedure - first lines of an emerging paradigm. Porto Alegre: Fabris Editor, 2004, p. 220; PORTO, Sergio Gilberto. **Comentarios ao Codigo de Processo Civil**. Sao Paulo: RT, 2000, v. 6, p. 222 and following; CABRAL, Antonio do Passo. **Coisa julgada e preclusoes dinamicas**. 2 ed. Salvador: Editora Jus Podivm, 2014, p. 95; STJ , 4ª Turma, REsp n°. 112.101/RS, rel. Min. Cesar Asfor Rocha, j. on 29.06.2000, published in the DJ of 18. 09.2000, p. 131.

[23] ASSIS, Araken de. **Cumulagao** de **agoes**. 4 ed. Sao Paulo: RT, 2002, p. 145 and 147; YOSHIKAWA, Eduardo Henrique de Oliveira. **The expansion of the preclusive efficacy of res judicata in matters of competition law**: considerations regarding art. 98, § 4, of the new CADE Law (Law 12.529/2011). Revista de Processo. Sao Paulo: RT, 2013, no. 222, p. 9496.

[24] TESHEINER, Jose Maria. **Efficacy of sentences and res judicata in civil proceedings**. Sao Paulo: RT, 2001, p. 161.

1.6 JUDICIAL MECHANISMS FOR CONTROLLING RES JUDICATA

A priori, our procedural system provides for the following judicial mechanisms to control res judicata:

a) the rescission action based on articles 966 et seq. of the CPC;

b) the *querela nullitatis based* on arts. 525, §1, I and 535, I, both of the CPC;

c) the challenge based on the existence of a material error under art. 494, I, of the CPC;

d) the review of an unconstitutional judgment based on articles 525, §12 and 535, I, both of the CPC;

e) also, according to some authors, the possibility of reforming res judicata on the grounds of a complaint of violation of the American Convention on Human Rights made before the Inter-American Court of Human Rights.[25]

As can be seen from the above list, there are judicial mechanisms that make res judicata more flexible in Brazilian civil proceedings, a characteristic that is more marked in criminal proceedings, where decisions of a material nature can be reviewed at any time in favor of the defendant; however, this is not repeated in favor of the State when it is transmuted as the prosecuting body. In short, it can be said that res judicata is not absolute.

The first to tackle the issue of the relativization of res judicata was the former minister of the STJ, Jose Augusto Delgado, who, after years of experience in concrete cases, preached that revision of the imperative burden of res judicata should be made possible when there is an affront to morality, legality, reasonableness and proportionality, or if it is far removed from the reality of the facts.

Other respected scholars follow the same line of thought, in the sense that res judicata should only remain unbreakable if: a) it complies with the

---

[25] TALAMINI, Eduardo. **The examination of Brazilian court judgments by the Inter-American Court of Human Rights**. In: Meios de Impugnapao ao julgado civil. Studies in Honor of Jose Carlos Barbosa Moreira. Adroaldo Furtado Fabricio (coord.). Rio de Janeiro: Forense, 2007.

maxims of proportionality, reasonableness and administrative morality - when it is not absurdly harmful to the state; b) it crystallizes the state's condemnation to pay "fair" amounts as compensation for real estate expropriation; c) it does not offend citizenship and human rights and does not violate the guarantee of an ecologically balanced environment.

On the other hand, many other scholars believe that allowing res judicata to be relativized using subjective criteria and allowing the judge to wander far afield from the typical procedural means that exist today, would open up the general power to review res judicata too much, generating various interpretations in concrete cases, which would certainly affect the legal certainty laid down in the Magna Carta, and what's more, would find resistance even in the substantive legislation itself in art. 505, II of the CPC, i.e. there would be no provision for reviewing res judicata by atypical criteria.

To think otherwise would be to deny the very essence of the Democratic State of Law, one of the pillars of which is the effectiveness of justice and regular access to the judiciary. In other words, there is no point in guaranteeing citizens access to the judiciary if they are not guaranteed the effectiveness and binding force of the decisions it makes.

Another point still up for debate is whether or not it is possible to relativize res judicata based on the unconstitutionality of the *decision,* since those in favor of this thesis maintain that the decision could be reviewed at any time, but it should not be forgotten that the principle of legal certainty also has constitutional status.

On the other hand, the procedural legislation in force provides a solution to this problem, with two basic ways of resolving the imbroglio: a) with the possibility of rescinding the sentence, based on item V of art. 966 of the CPC, mitigating the rigor of Sumula 343 of the STF; b) the provision of §12 of art. 525 and §5 of art. 535 of the CPC.

In a different vein, however, the STF allowed the renewal of a paternity investigation claim that had previously been rejected due to lack of evidence, thus establishing a case of relativization of res judicata. Even without expressly saying so, the STF considered res judicata in paternity investigations to be *secundum eventum probationis* (RE n. 363.889, king. Min. Dias Toffoli, j. 02.06.2011).

The Superior Court of Justice has also admitted the atypical revision of res judicata in the case of expropriation, by means of a petition filed in the execution proceedings, on the grounds of illegitimacy *ad causam* or injustice in the amount of compensation (STJ, 1ª T. REsp 62.2405/SP, rel. Min. Denise Arruda, j. 14.08.2007, published in the DJ of 20.09.2007, p. 221).

Weighing up the arguments of both currents, one cannot help but express concern about the possibility of re-discussing res judicata based on allegations of injustice or disproportionality from a constitutional point of view, since the constitutional principle of legal certainty must always be kept in mind, and the exceptions to res judicata are very clear in the infra-constitutional legislation.

2 PROVISIONAL PROTECTION

2.1 BASIC NOTIONS

2.1.1 Definitive guardianship: types

Before moving on to the specific subject of this chapter, it is important to note that the jurisdictional protection provided for in current procedural legislation is divided into two: definitive protection and provisional protection.

There is no escaping the fact that provisional relief is the relief that is intended to be final at the end of the legal action. Definitive relief is obtained after an in-depth procedural debate, in which the parties are guaranteed due process of law, the adversarial process, a broad defense and other constitutional and infra-constitutional legal constraints, the decision of which is predisposed to be crystallized by the institute of res judicata.

The first aims to give effectiveness to the material right, also called standard protection by Teori Zavascki[26] , which is divided into certification protection (declaratory, constitutive and condemnatory) and the protection of the effectiveness of rights (executive protection); the second does not aim to satisfy a right, but to ensure future satisfaction, to preserve the right claimed and neutralize the negative effects of time.

2.1.2 Injunctive relief

As seen above, injunctive relief is distinguished from satisfactory relief not only because they have different motives, but also because they have two *sui generis* characteristics, i.e. referability and temporariness.

> Precautionary protection is a means of preserving another right, the right being protected, which is the object of satisfactory protection. Precautionary

[26] ZAVASCKI, Teori Albino. **Antecipação de Tutela**. 2 ed. Sao Paulo: Saraiva, 1999, p. 18-21.

> protection is necessarily a protection that refers to another right, distinct from the right to the precaution itself. There is the right to precaution and the right to be cautioned. The right to precaution is the right to precautionary protection; the right that is being protected, or the right that is being protected, is the right that is the subject of the precautionary protection. This reference is essential.[27]

In addition to its referability, injunctive relief is also temporary, since its effectiveness is limited in time. In other words, once it has fulfilled its protective function, it soon loses its effectiveness.

Normally, precautionary protection loses its practical effects at the exact moment when its beneficiary obtains definitive satisfaction of their right, or rather, when they succeed in resolving the main claim in which the right being protected is being discussed or and/or enforced.

Ovidio Baptista da Silva makes a good distinction between the provisional and the temporary:

> The temporary is always intended to be "exchanged" for the definitive, which is of the same nature - e.g. the temporary "apartment" in which the couple lives, to be replaced by the definitive dwelling (apartment in a building under construction). What is temporary is definitive, nothing will replace it (of the same nature), but its effects are limited in time, and predisposed to cessation - e.g. scaffolding put up to paint the building in which the couple will live will remain there for as long as it takes to complete the job (once the job is done, they will leave, but nothing will replace them).[28]

In short, injunctive relief is temporary, but it is not provisional, because no other guarantee measure will come along to replace it, it will only be the guarantee for the effectiveness of the right sought in the main claim, which, when it comes to an end, will carry with it the temporary effects of the injunctive relief, but even though it is finite, it is still definitive for the purposes it is intended (guaranteeing the certification or effectiveness of the substantive right).

---

[27] DIDIER JR, Fredie; BRAGA, Paula Sarno; OLIVEIRA, Rafael Alexandria de. **Civil Procedure Course**. 10 ed., Bahia: Editora Jus PODIVM, 2015, v. 2, p. 562-563.

[28] BAPTISTA DA SILVA, Ovidio. **Precautionary Process**. 3 ed. Rio de Janeiro: Forense, 2006, p. 86.

2.1.3 Immutability (res judicata) of injunctive relief

As stated above, although the precautionary protection order is temporary, there is no way of removing its definitive nature.

In addition, precautionary protection, like any act of applying to the courts, has a method to be followed which must be made up of a request for the guarantee (security) of a right and also a cause of action based on a remote plausibility of the right to be protected and, in addition, a demonstration of the danger of delay; finally, the actual demonstration of the right to precaution.

In order to grant injunctive relief, the material right of which is to be protected summarily, the judge must base himself on the probability of the right invoked (certification or effectiveness), exactly in terms of the requirement of *fumus boni iuris.*

> The probability of the right (traditionally called "fumus boni iuris") is an element of the factual support for the right to precautionary protection. In other words: as we shall see, in order for the right to precautionary protection of another right to be recognized, it is necessary to show that this other right, or the right being protected, is probable. Once this factual support (probability of the right being protected) has been realized, the right to precautionary protection can be definitively certified.[29]

The task to be accomplished by those who wish to protect their rights is to demonstrate to the judge the likelihood of their right and especially that the passage of time could cause them discomfort, either with the perishing of the very right sought in the main claim or the diminution of what can be achieved in the end.

> Having a factual support made up of probability or plausibility does not imply that the right that derives from it cannot be recognized in a decision based on exaurient cognition. This is the cognitive depth that must be reached in order for the right to precaution to be recognized: the probability of the right being protected. The doctrine points to other subjective rights that are based on factual assumptions integrated by the

[32] DIDIER JR, Fredie; BRAGA, Paula Sarno; OLIVEIRA, Rafael Alexandria de. **Course on Civil Procedure**. 10 ed., Bahia: Editora Jus PODIVM, 2015, v. 2, p. 568.

probability. This is true of the right to compensation for loss of profits, which is based on the probability of profit, and the rights of the unborn child, which are based on the probability that it will be born alive.[30]

In order for the precautionary order to be granted, the magistrate must recognize that two basic assumptions have been met: the likelihood of the right being protected and the danger of delay, in relation to which (the right being protected) cognition will be summary, but in relation to the right to precaution, it will obviously be exaurient: "Thus, if there is a precautionary decision on the merits, with exaurient cognition, and no longer subject to appeal, there is res judicata."[31]

In this line of reasoning, it can be concluded that injunctive relief is final if it is not attacked in due course through the appropriate procedural mechanisms, which makes it immutable, so its temporary nature is only for practical purposes, in other words, injunctive relief only loses its effects when the right it protects is recognized and satisfied or when the right is not recognized in the main claim, however, the decision that granted it remains intact from a technical point of view.

The sole paragraph of art. 309 of the CPC in force sums up the issue very well when it states that the content of the final precautionary decision can no longer be altered, not even if new facts emerge, but nothing prevents a new precautionary claim from being brought based on new grounds:

> Art. 309. The effectiveness of a preliminary injunction shall cease if:
> [...]
> Sole paragraph. If the effectiveness of the precautionary measure ceases for any reason, the party may not renew the request, except on new grounds.

It is clear that a precautionary order that has not been modified

[30] COSTA, Eduardo Jose da Fonseca. **Precautionary sentence, cognition and res judicata** - reflections in honor of the memory of Ovidio Baptista. Revista de Processo. Sao Paulo: RT, 2011, no. 191, p. 368.
[31] COSTA, *op.cit.,* 2011, p. 365.

[32] DIDIER JR, Fredie; BRAGA, Paula Sarno; OLIVEIRA, Rafael Alexandria de. **Course on Civil Procedure**. 10 ed., Bahia: Editora Jus PODIVM, 2015, v. 2, p. 568.

through the appropriate procedural means is immutable, even preventing it from being re-discussed at a later date, but if a new situation arises on different grounds, it can be revived.

2.2 PROVISIONAL ADVANCE OF THE EFFECTS OF THE FINAL INJUNCTION

2.2.1 General guidelines

The issue is highly controversial and also touches on the structures and paradigms of the current process, because on the one hand, no one can imagine a judge making immediate decisions based on "guesswork", more typical of imperialist periods when decisions are centralized in a few or just one person.

Today, the issue of time and the effectiveness of definitive judicial protection will have to be dealt with in a very balanced way, but without forgetting the legal constraints of a judicial process permeated with procedural and constitutional guarantees, especially guaranteeing the parties the right to lodge appeals and have judicial decisions re-evaluated by higher courts.

On the other hand, the usefulness of the process must also be taken into account, since the passing of time naturally makes the parties' interest in the judicial outcome cool or even makes any interest disappear, not least because it is not uncommon for the parties to spend a lifetime litigating and in the end have no strength left to enjoy the practical outcome of the lawsuit.

As a result, the new CPC has introduced a new chapter dealing with interim relief, which aims to guarantee the practical effectiveness of the main claim, such as guaranteeing the satisfaction of the winner's assets by preventing the debtor from squandering his assets.

[32] DIDIER JR, Fredie; BRAGA, Paula Sarno; OLIVEIRA, Rafael Alexandria de. **Course on Civil Procedure**. 10 ed., Bahia: Editora Jus PODIVM, 2015, v. 2, p. 568.

Thinking about the two hypotheses (urgency and evidentiary), in the first case provisional injunctive relief balances the time needed to resolve the procedural conflict and its effectiveness over time, in the second case there is no urgency, but the party's (proven) right is so evident that it cannot withstand the time needed to grant definitive injunctive relief.

Book V of the current CPC provides for provisional protection in order to mitigate the negative effects of time in the process and ensure that the final result is effective, i.e. can be used by the holder of the right, whether from a satisfactory or precautionary point of view.

Furthermore, provisional protection aims to divide the responsibility for the passage of time between the litigants in a court case, where the debtor who uses countless appeals to delay the satisfaction of his debt has his assets made unavailable, for example, while the creditor has the expectation of satisfying his claim at the end of the litigation, preventing the debtor from squandering his assets.

> This is anticipatory relief, referred to in the CPC-2015 as "provisional relief". Interim relief provides prompt satisfaction or assurance. The decision granting interim relief is based on summary cognizance and gives immediate effect to the final relief sought (satisfactory or precautionary). Because it is provisional, it will be replaced by a definitive order that confirms, revokes or modifies it.[32]

However, if the plaintiff's intention is to seek satisfactory interim relief granted in advance, coupled with the defendant's lack of interest or inertia, the process will not necessarily follow the regular path to satisfaction via definitive relief, and the procedural confrontation may be over, with the plaintiff being satisfied and also the defendant not opposing the proposed anticipation.

[32] DIDIER JR, Fredie; BRAGA, Paula Sarno; OLIVEIRA, Rafael Alexandria de. **Course on Civil Procedure**. 10 ed., Bahia: Editora Jus PODIVM, 2015, v. 2, p. 568.

2.2.2 Peculiarities

Interim protection has three outstanding characteristics, one of which will be the basis of this paper's discussion.

According to the doctrine, summary cognition is the first characteristic, authorizing the judge to superficially analyze the litigious matter and decide based on a judgment of probability.

A characteristic of this procedural modality is its precariousness, since its effectiveness over time is subject to the possibility of a new judicial decision, based on a new fact (fact, law or state of the evidence), to the contrary, as prescribed in art. 290 of the CPC.

Adding the two characteristics above, the third arises, the one that is of interest as the basis of this study, because the decision is based on summary and precarious cognition, it would be inapt to make it indisputable by res judicata, however, if its granting is not questioned, we are facing the phenomenon of stabilization provided for in art. 304 of the CPC, when in particular there is the inertia or failure of the defendant to oppose the provisional guardianship granted.

The last chapter will discuss the similarities or dissimilarities between res judicata and the stabilization of interim relief.

2.2.3 Types of interim relief: satisfactory (advance) and precautionary

The difference between the two forms of interim relief is quite striking, especially because satisfactory interim relief can only be granted when it is the future claim for definitive relief, i.e. the types of definitive relief are, therefore, the types of interim relief.[33]

[32] DIDIER JR, Fredie; BRAGA, Paula Sarno; OLIVEIRA, Rafael Alexandria de. **Course on Civil Procedure**. 10 ed., Bahia: Editora Jus PODIVM, 2015, v. 2, p. 568.

Satisfactory interim relief anticipates the effects of definitive relief, immediately delivering the right sought by the plaintiff.

> Precautionary injunctions thus have a dual function: they are provisional in that they give immediate effect to non-satisfactory definitive injunctions; and they are precautionary in that they ensure the future effectiveness of satisfactory definitive injunctions, insofar as they safeguard the right to be satisfied.[34]

Precautionary injunctions, on the other hand, advance the effects of non-satisfactory (precautionary) definitive injunctions, giving immediate effect to the right to precaution. What is advanced in this type of provisional protection is the immediate preservation of the right to be protected, guaranteeing the future satisfaction of the main claim (definitive protection).

2.2.4 Requirements

According to article 294 of the Civil Procedure Code, provisional protection can be based on urgency or evidence:

> Art. 294. Provisional relief may be based on urgency or evidence.
> Sole paragraph. Provisional, precautionary or advance injunctive relief may be granted on an antecedent or incidental basis.

Emergency measures - precautionary and satisfactory - are based on the common requirements of *fumus boni iuris* and *periculum in mora.* There is no longer a distinction between a precautionary application based on the appearance of good law and an anticipatory application based on unequivocal evidence.

However, it is still very important to differentiate between precautionary and satisfactory protection, as Humberto Theodoro Jr. teaches:

> (i) the precautionary measure's subsistence is always dependent on the procedure which, in the end, will have to settle the litigation which can be called "main", or "on the merits"; while (ii) the advance injunction can, at the convenience of the parties, be stabilized, dispensing with the need to continue with the procedure in order to reach the final judgment on the

[34] *Id.*

> merits, and, therefore, without the formation of res judicata. In other words: the precautionary measure, because it restricts the right, without giving any composition to the litigation, cannot be stabilized, outside or independently of the definitive judicial rendering; only the measure of advance guardianship can, eventually, be stabilized, because in it a summary composition of the litigation is obtained, with which the litigants can be satisfied.[35]

The requirements for obtaining provisional injunctive relief are: (a) potential damage, a risk that the process will not be useful to the interest demonstrated by the party, due to the *periculum in mora, a* risk that must be objectively ascertainable; *(b) the probability of the substantial right* invoked by the person seeking security, in other words, the *fumus boni iuris.*[36]

It's good to make it clear that urgency can be the basis for granting precautionary or satisfactory interim relief, however, evidence only authorizes satisfactory interim relief[37] , in other words, in order to request satisfactory interim relief, it is necessary to allege and prove urgency or evidence or both; however, precautionary interim relief is only necessary to allege and prove urgency.

2.2.5 When to apply for interim relief

It is clear from the new CPC that provisional injunctive relief can be sought both in advance and incidentally; on the other hand, provisional injunctive relief can only be sought incidentally (art. 294, p. unico): "In addition to being granted in limine or after the defendant has been heard, 'provisional injunctive relief' can also be used throughout the common procedure and even in the judgment itself."[38]

It may also happen that the urgency is contemporaneous with the filing of the lawsuit, but because of the complexity of the main lawsuit, the volume of

[35] THEODORO Jr., Humberto. **Civil Procedure Course**. 56 ed. Rio de Janeiro: Forense, 2015, vol. 1, p. 619.
[36] THEODORO, *op. cit,* 2016, p. 620.
[37] COSTA, Eduardo Jose da Fonseca. **Guardianship of evidence in the New CPC Project - an analysis of its presuppositions**. The future of

Civil Procedure in Brazil - a critical analysis of the draft new CPC. Belo Horizonte: Forum, 2011, p. 171, note 8.
[38] MARINONI, Luiz Guilherme; ARENHART, Sergio Cruz; MITIDIERO, Daniel. **Civil Procedure Course**. Sao Paulo: RT, 2015, vol. 2, p. 208.

documents and evidence to be gathered, or even if the plaintiff does not have time to postpone his provisional claim, be it satisfactory or precautionary, in these cases the new Code allows the plaintiff, at first, to limit himself to the request for advance relief and the indication of the request for final relief, with an exposition of the dispute, the right that is being sought and the danger of damage or risk to the useful result of the process (art. 303).

In summary: urgent relief can be requested at three different times: *(a)* before the main claim is filed (antecedent relief); *(b)* in the initial application for the main action (cumulative relief); and *(c) in the* course of the main proceedings (incidental relief).

2.3 PROVISIONAL INJUNCTIONS

2.3.1 Basics

As has already been seen, provisional injunctive relief can be precautionary or satisfactory, and in both cases it is necessary for the applicant to demonstrate *periculum in mora* and *fumus boni iuris* (Statement No. 143 of the Permanent Forum of Civil Proceduralists).

It's important to reproduce Eduardo Jose da Fonseca Costa's links:

> The *fumus boni iuris* and the *periculum in mora* are seen as 'movable' guidelines, which can present themselves in different degrees or levels and which, for this reason, are not susceptible to being fixed in general terms (...) Consequently, in order to grant the preliminary injunction, there is no need for the two presuppositions to be present simultaneously. There is a kind of free interchangeability between them. If the specific case deviates from the 'normal type' and only one of the presuppositions is present in 'decisive weight', it will still be possible to grant the measure, albeit by virtue of an 'atypical' or 'less typical' configuration, which deviates from the model described in the law. Everything happens as if, in the concrete processes of granting injunctions, *fumus boni iuris* and *periculum in mora* were 'elements' or 'forces' that are articulated in a variable way, without absolutism and

dimensional fixity".[35]

The probability of the right alleged must be based on elements that show the possibility of what has been narrated having happened and what the plaintiff's chances of success are.

With regard to the danger of delay, it is well drawn and easy to understand, consisting of the need to prove the danger of damage (concrete, current and serious) or risk to the useful outcome of the process.

The fact is that we may not always be facing a situation of irreparable damage or damage that is difficult to repair, but we may be facing a fear arising from an act that is contrary to the law (unlawful).

There are situations in which the damage has already occurred, so the plaintiff has applied for permanent injunctive relief, such as: injunction, reinstatement or compensation; nothing prevents them from also applying for provisional injunctive relief, whether precautionary or satisfactory, for example, to remove their name from the credit protection service, to delete an offensive post on a social network, etc.

Satisfactory provisional injunctive relief also requires proof of the possibility of reversing the effects of the anticipatory decision (art. 300, §3, CPC), because if it is not confirmed in the end, it is crucial to return to the *status quo ante,* without causing damage to the opposing party.

In this vein, several scholars warn that this requirement should not be taken lightly, otherwise the possibility of provisional protection would fall apart, and its interpretation should be softened. In such situations, it is up to the judge to weigh up the values at stake, giving protection to the one which, in the specific case, is most important.[36]

Another measure commonly taken by magistrates and provided for in

---

[35] COSTA, Eduardo Jose da Fonseca. **Guardianship of evidence in the New CPC Project - an analysis of its presuppositions**. The future of Civil Procedure in Brazil - a critical analysis of the draft new CPC. Belo Horizonte: Forum, 2011, p. 169.

[36] MIRANDA NETO, Fernando Gama de. **A ponderapao de interesses na tutela de urgência irreversivel**. Rio de Janeiro: Lumen Juris, 2005, p. 142 - 157.

the new CPC is the requirement of a bond for the granting of satisfactory interim relief (art. 300, §1).

It is crucial to point out that all provisional measures of urgency, whether precautionary or satisfactory, can be requested incidentally or in advance, and that it is the latter type (satisfactory provisional measures of urgency, granted in advance) that is of most interest at the moment, because it brings the possibility of stabilizing the judicial decision in the event of inertia or acquiescence by the defendant, the effects of which we intend to compare with res judicata in the final chapter.

2.4 DIFFERENCE BETWEEN (ADVANCE) INJUNCTIVE RELIEF GRANTED IN ADVANCE AND PRECAUTIONARY INJUNCTIVE RELIEF GRANTED IN ADVANCE

2.4.1 Preliminary injunctions for urgent relief

Precedent satisfactory (advance) injunctive relief is that which takes place within the process in which the final injunction will be requested in the future, but, due to its urgency represented by the *periculum in mora* and *fumus boni iures, it is* allowed to be requested before the final injunction is requested.

The contemporary CPC sets out a proper procedure for its implementation, specifically in art. 303 et seq, which must be accompanied by the following requirements:

> The situation of urgency, which already exists at the time the action is filed, justifies the plaintiff limiting himself to the following in the initial petition:
> a) request a preliminary injunction;
> b) indicate the request for final injunctive relief - which will be made within the time limit laid down by law for the amendment;
> c) set out the dispute, the right that is being sought (and its probability), and the danger of delay (art. 303, caput, CPC);
> d) indicate the value of the cause, taking into account the request for definitive relief that it intends to formulate (art. 303, §4, CPC); and, finally,

> f) explain that you intend to make use of the benefit of applying for preliminary injunctions, in accordance with the *heading of* art. 303, CPC (art. 303, § 5, CPC).[41]

Based on the dynamics presented above, there will be two paths to follow, since provisional protection may or may not be granted by the judge; if it is not granted because its presuppositions are not present, the judge will order the plaintiff to amend the initial petition within the time limit set by law (5 days), under penalty of having the case dismissed without a decision on the merits (art. 303, § 6, CPC). 303, § 6, CPC); if the provisional relief sought is granted, the magistrate will have to take another route, as provided for in art. 303, §§ 1, 2 and 3, of the CPC, i.e. he must order the plaintiff to amend the initial application within a period of not less than 15 days, under the same penalty of termination of the proceedings without resolution on the merits. In addition, the judge will also order the defendant to be summoned to comply with the measure granted by way of interim relief and also to attend the conciliation or mediation hearing.

> Art. 303. In cases where the urgency is contemporaneous with the filing of the action, the initial petition may be limited to the request for advance relief and the indication of the request for final relief, with an exposition of the dispute, the right sought to be realized and the danger of damage or risk to the useful outcome of the proceedings.
> § Paragraph 1. Once the preliminary injunction referred to in the main section of this article has been granted:
> I - the plaintiff must add to the initial petition, supplementing his arguments, attaching new documents and confirming the request for final injunctive relief, within 15 (fifteen) days or such longer period as the judge may set;
> II - the defendant shall be summoned to the conciliation or mediation hearing in accordance with art. 334;
> III - If there is no self-composition, the time limit for contesting will be counted in accordance with art. 335.
> § Paragraph 2. If the amendment referred to in item I of paragraph 1 of this article is not made, the case shall be dismissed without a decision on the merits.
> § Paragraph 3. The amendment referred to in item I of Paragraph 1 of this article shall be made in the same case file, without incurring new procedural costs.
> [...]

[38] DIDIER JR, Fredie; BRAGA, Paula Sarno; OLIVEIRA, Rafael Alexandria de. **Course on Civil Procedure**. 10 ed., Bahia: Editora Jus PODIVM, 2015, v. 2, p. 602-603.

If the parties reach an agreement, the claim will be settled in accordance with art. 334 of the CPC. However, if the judicial impasse continues, the deadline for contesting the claim will only start to run once the defendant has been informed of the amendment to the initial claim submitted by the plaintiff, which does not require a new writ of summons and can be sent via the defendant's lawyer, and the ordinary procedure with all its phases (sanitation, investigation and decision) will begin.

On the other hand, if the defendant is summoned and notified of the granting of the provisional injunction and remains inert, i.e. does not contest or appeal the decision, he will be faced with the problematic issue of this work called the stabilization of the decision of the preliminary injunction and consequently the extinction of the case.

What's more, it's also crucial to state that the type of provisional injunctive relief will not have the same effects as the first, in other words, it will not experience the effects of stabilization.

2.4.2 Preliminary injunctive relief

This type of provisional protection is the starting point for a future request for definitive protection, the main purpose of which is to provisionally advance the effectiveness of the definitive precautionary protection and also to ensure the future effectiveness of the definitive satisfactory protection.[42]

The new CPC provides for a specific procedure, as set out in art. 305 et seq:

> a) a request for provisional injunctive relief, on an antecedent basis - to be confirmed on a definitive basis - where appropriate, either as a preliminary injunction or with prior justification (art. 300, § 2, CPC); b) an indication of the dispute, its grounds and a summary statement of the probability

[39] DIDIER JR, Fredie; BRAGA, Paula Sarno; OLIVEIRA, Rafael Alexandria de. **Course on Civil Procedure**. 10 ed., Bahia: Editora Jus PODIVM, 2015, v. 2, p. 602-603.

of the right sought to be protected; and c) demonstration of the danger of delay (art. 305 et seq., CPC).[43]

Once the initial application is complete, the judge may, of course, reject or grant the request, and in the second case he may do so without hearing the opposing party or with prior justification. If the preliminary injunction is granted, the judge must order that it be complied with and that the defendant be summoned to contest the application and specify any evidence he intends to produce (art. 306, CPC).

On the other hand, if the defendant does not contest the claim - which is different from the stabilizing effects of uncontested preliminary injunctions - default will be established and the effects of art. 344 of the CPC will apply. If the claim is contested, the ordinary procedure will begin.

Another characteristic of preliminary injunctive relief is the need for the plaintiff to carry out the measure. If the plaintiff does not do so within 30 days, it is presumed that the risks and the party's own interest in the precautionary measure have disappeared (art. 309, II, CPC), however, external factors that do not allow the measure to be carried out within this period cannot prejudice the plaintiff's right (slowness of the Judiciary, delaying measures by the defendant, etc.).

As soon as the precautionary measure is complied with/enforced, the 30-day period begins to run for the plaintiff to file the main claim and add the definitive cause of action. The main claim must be made within the time limit set in the event of the precautionary measure being granted or rejected, and no new procedural costs are required (art. 308, CPC).

Once the plaintiff has formulated the main request, the judge will appoint a conciliation or mediation hearing (art. 334, CPC), with no need for a new summons. If no agreement is reached between the parties, the defendant may contest the precautionary application within 15 days, at which point the process is subject to the ritualistic rules of ordinary procedure.

---

[43] *id.*

It is important to emphasize the independence of injunctive relief from final injunctive relief, since the outcome of the former does not influence the outcome of the latter.

> Even when the precautionary measure has not been granted, the party may formulate its "main request", the judgment of which will not be influenced by this - unless the grounds for rejecting the precautionary measure are prescription or decay of the right being protected (art. 310, CPC).[44]
> Precautionary injunctions, as has been seen, are autonomous from satisfactory injunctions and have their own merits (request and cause of action). This autonomy also stands out when one realizes that the outcome of the precautionary claim does not influence the outcome of the satisfactory claim. The person who wins the precautionary measure can win the main claim and vice versa. The preliminary injunction is granted or dismissed on its own merits and not on the merits of the main claim.[45]

Finally, once the final injunction has been judged, whether the claim has been upheld or dismissed, the effects of the precautionary measure will cease, in the first case when the right which is the subject of the action has been fully satisfied, in the second case for obvious reasons, as laid down in art. 309, III, of the CPC. It is worth remembering that once the effectiveness of a precautionary measure has ceased for whatever reason, it cannot be sought again, except as a result of new facts (art. 309, sole paragraph).

Another point to highlight is the possibility for the judge to grant satisfactory relief in place of the precautionary relief requested by the plaintiff, in other words, the legislator itself provided for the fungibility of emergency relief in art. 305, sole paragraph of the CPC, however, there is no express provision in the law for the reverse possibility, that is, to grant precautionary relief to the detriment of the satisfactory relief previously requested by the plaintiff.

Despite some discussions about whether or not the judge can convert the measure requested into the most appropriate one for the specific case, the doctrine has been in favor of fungibility in both directions, either progressively or regressively:

---

[44] THEODORO JR., Humberto. **Processo Cautelar**. 22 ed. Sao Paulo: Leud, 2005, p. 158.
[45] THEODORO JR., *ibid.,* 2005, p. 56 and 59.

> Thus, art. 305, sole paragraph, CPC, provides that, once a precautionary measure has been requested in an antecedent nature, if the judge considers that it is of a satisfactory nature (anticipatory), he may receive it, provided that he follows the corresponding procedure. This is a case of progressive fungibility, of converting the precautionary measure into a satisfactory one, i.e. from the least aggressive to the most aggressive. If the legislator admits this progressive fungibility (from precautionary to satisfactory), then by analogy, regressive fungibility from satisfactory to precautionary (from the most to the least aggressive and rigorous) must be admitted. In this way, once a satisfactory provisional (advance) injunction has been applied for, if the judge considers that it is of a precautionary nature, he or she may grant it, provided that he or she follows the procedure laid down by law. The decision must be clearly motivated in this regard, not least so that the defendant is aware of the consequences of his inaction, which are far more serious if the request is for satisfactory interim relief.[46]

We have now considered the two types of injunctive relief that can be granted in advance, especially pointing out that the phenomenon of stabilization only occurs in antecedent satisfactory (advance) injunctive relief.

2.5 PROVISIONAL PROTECTION OF EVIDENCE

2.5.1 Basics

Guardianship of evidence, unlike other provisional guardianships, is not based on the situation that generates a danger of damage, but on immediate proof of the party's sufficient right.

Evidence is a procedural legal fact. It is the procedural state in which statements of fact are proven.[47]

Guardianship of evidence is justified by the possibility of ascertaining the liquidity and certainty of the material right alleged, even if it cannot be granted definitively, but by the fact that sufficient elements of conviction have been gathered for the judge, he can anticipate the right sought by the plaintiff, however, this does not mean that the procedural clash is over and much less that it is an early judgment of the case.

[46] DIDIER JR, Fredie; BRAGA, Paula Sarno; OLIVEIRA, Rafael Alexandria de. **Civil Procedure Course**. 10 ed., Bahia: Editora Jus PODIVM, 2015, v. 2, p. 615-616.

[47] FUX, Luiz. Guardianship of **Security and Guardianship of Evidence**. Sao Paulo: Saraiva, 1996, p. 311 and 313.

Guardianship of evidence seeks to balance the negative effects of time in resolving the dispute, when the circumstances of the case and the evidence authorize one of the parties to be delivered/satisfied, because the passage of time may cause them harm, and definitive guardianship will prove useless.

The provisional nature of injunctive relief is undeniable, as is that of urgent relief, even though in many cases the granting of such relief means the early delivery of definitive relief, a fact that does not prevent the continuation of the investigation and judgment of the case, which may ultimately be denied and the injunctive relief granted in advance revoked.

Evidence is characterized by the coexistence of two presuppositions: proof of the factual allegations and the likelihood of the procedural claim being accepted. In this form of protection, there is no need to demonstrate urgency or danger of damage, since its primary objective is to redistribute the burden of time for the procedural outcome between the parties, handing over the material right in advance to those who provide robust proof of it and demonstrate the likelihood of success at the end of the dispute.

> Its aim is to redistribute the burden that comes with the time it takes for a lawsuit to pass and for a definitive injunction to be granted. This is done by granting immediate and provisional relief to the party who reveals the high degree of probability of their allegations (duly proven), to the detriment of the opposing party and the unlikelihood of success in their resistance - even after a procedural investigation.[48]

This type of provisional protection finds its guiding rule in the CF/88 itself, in its article 5, item LXXVIII: "everyone, in the judicial and administrative spheres, is guaranteed a reasonable duration of the process and the means to ensure that it is dealt with swiftly"; this being the case, there is nothing more appropriate than delivering the right that is evident in the one that shows the greatest chance of future success.

Nor should it be forgotten that the immediate delivery of the plaintiff's claim discourages the defendant and reduces his procedural resistance, a situation that will greatly contribute to the outcome of the case, including the

[48] BODART, Bruno Vinicius de Ros. **Guardianship of Evidence**. Sao Paulo: RT, 2014, p. 132.

possibility of using alternative mechanisms to resolve the conflict.

Another characteristic of injunctive relief is that it presupposes the main claim has already been filed, since it is through this that the judge will be able to analyze the evidence and proof of the right claimed, together with the latent possibility of success in the end. However, there is nothing to prevent injunctive relief from also being requested on an incidental basis (art. 311, I, of the CPC).

For this reason, the doctrine usually classifies provisional injunctions of evidence into two types:

a) punitive (art. 311, I), when the "abuse of the right of defense or the manifest intent to delay on the part of the party" is characterized;

b) documented, when there is documentary proof of the party's allegations of fact, in the hypotheses of art. 311, II to IV, which determine the likelihood of the procedural claim being accepted. Its assumptions will be analyzed below.

Having made the necessary distinctions between the two types of injunctive relief and evidentiary relief, we now move on to analyze the phenomenon of stabilization typical of antecedent satisfactory (advance) injunctive relief.

3 STABILIZATION OF SATISFACTORY (ADVANCE) INJUNCTIONS - SIMILARITIES AND DISSIMILARITIES WITH RES JUDICATA

3.1 BASIC NOTES

The current Civil Procedure Code followed the evolutionary line of summary relief already outlined in Italian and Trance law, admitting the disconnection between summary injunctive relief and full injunctive relief or merits proceedings, in other words, it allowed the so-called autonomization and stabilization of summary relief[49] , which is also called the technique of monitoring civil proceedings .[50]

> In a departure from the traditional design of injunctive relief, the Brazilian legislator innovated by making the summary judgment that leads to the granting of injunctive relief procedurally autonomous (art. 303). In a word: it made advance relief *autonomous*. This is an option whose main objective is to make it possible to introduce the mechanism of *stabilization of preliminary injunctions* in Brazilian law (art. 304).[51]

It is also justified to call the stabilization of the preliminary injunction a monitoring technique, since there is a generalization of the monitoring technique already used in the old *Codex,* which makes it possible to obtain practical results from the inertia of the defendant.

> Under the CPC-1973 regime, the monitoring technique was used as part of a special procedure aimed at protecting rights to a payment (to pay a sum of money and to deliver a fungible thing or a certain movable thing) documented in written evidence that was not enforceable (art. 1.102-A ss., CPC-1973) - i.e. evident rights to payment. Once the initial application has been duly instructed in these terms, the judge, by means of a still summary cognition, could issue a warrant ordering the defendant to comply with the obligation within fifteen days or to defend himself with a motion to stay the proceedings. Once the objections have been offered, the ordinary procedure will proceed to form an exhaustive judgment. If the objections are

[49] THEODORO Jr., Humberto. **Civil Procedure Course**. 56 ed. Rio de Janeiro: Forense, 2015, vol. 1, p. 674.

[50] DIDIER JR, Fredie; BRAGA, Paula Sarno; OLIVEIRA, Rafael Alexandria de. **Civil Procedure Course**. 10 ed., Bahia: Editora Jus PODIVM, 2015, v. 2, p. 604.

[51] MARINONI, Luiz Guilherme; ARENHART, Sergio Cruz; MITIDIERO, Daniel. **Civil Procedure Course**. Sao Paulo: RT, 2015, vol. 2, p. 207.

> not offered within the time limit (or if they are rejected), the decision that initially ordered the issuance of a writ to enforce the obligation would become enforceable, assuming the status of a judicial enforcement order."[52] . In other words, if the defendant is inert in the face of the evidence of the plaintiff's right ascertained by summary cognition, the plaintiff is given an executive title that authorizes the immediate and rapid enforcement of his right. Articles 700 et seq. of the CPC maintain this special procedure, with a few adjustments. The monitoring action is extended, for example, to rights to a performance of a duty to do or not to do.[53]

In this case, the satisfactory relief decision is stabilized when it is granted in advance and is not challenged by the defendant, co-partner or simple assistant, either through an appeal or another means of challenge. If the interested parties fail to act, the case will be dismissed and the decision will continue to produce its effects until the interested party files an independent action to review, reform or invalidate it.

As the satisfactory relief decision is granted in advance, it does not go into the main claim, therefore, as far as it is concerned, there is no decision resolving the merits, not least because the main claim was not even formulated (it was only mentioned), if it coexisted with the main claim there would be an incidental claim for satisfactory relief.

3.2 CONDITIONS FOR THE STABILIZATION OF INJUNCTIVE RELIEF GRANTED IN ADVANCE

As established by the rules on the subject (art. 304, *caput* and § 1, CPC), it is up to the defendant, if he does not want the satisfactory protection granted in advance to be stabilized, to file the appropriate appeal against the decision - *in this case, an interlocutory* appeal -, *in* addition to the fact that the case is terminated without judgment on the merits.

---

[52] TALAMINI, Eduardo. **Tutela Monitoria**. 2 ed. Sao Paulo: RT, 2001, p. 92 and ss, *apud* DIDIER; BRAGA e OLIVEIRA, *op. cit.* 2015, p. 604 - 605.
[53] *id.*

It should be noted that a simple reading of the procedural provision mentioned above leads us to the first impression that the only way to avoid stabilizing the preliminary injunction in question would be to use the interlocutory appeal, but as will be seen later in this study, there are doctrinal positions for the most varied tastes.

In addition, it is worth remembering that the legislator was motivated by two basic objectives in constructing this procedural technique, in particular to ward off the malevolent effects of time in the process, mitigating the danger of delay in providing justice, and also to offer the plaintiff effective and immediate results in the face of any delay on the part of the defendant.[54]

In order for the stabilization of satisfactory injunctive relief granted in advance to materialize, a number of conditions must be met:

a) that the plaintiff makes the request in the initial petition to avail himself of the benefit of the preliminary injunction, in accordance with art. 303, § 5 of the CPC, which indicates that he has an interest in its stabilization;

b) that there is no request in the initial petition for preliminary injunctive relief for the continuation of the proceedings after the relief sought has been granted;

c) obviously, that there is a positive decision regarding the granting of antecedent satisfactory relief; and

d) there is no challenge from the defendant, passive co-conspirator or simple assistant, by means of a proper appeal or other means of challenging the respective decision, in addition, it is stated in the legal text that there will also be no stabilization when the defendant is summoned in a fictitious manner, is imprisoned or incapacitated and is not legitimately represented.

[54] DIDIER JR, Fredie; BRAGA, Paula Sarno; OLIVEIRA, Rafael Alexandria de. **Course on Civil Procedure**. 10 ed., Bahia: Editora Jus PODIVM, 2015, v. 2, p. 606.

3.2.1 Time for the plaintiff to comment on the continuation of the main action

As seen above, one of the preconditions for the granting of preliminary injunctive relief is that the plaintiff makes an express request about his intention, as it would be clear that there is an interest in stabilizing the decision.

With this in mind, the doctrine has demanded that the request for the continuation or not of the main proceedings be evident in the initial petition for urgent relief, because in the event of the preliminary injunction being granted, it will guide the defendant's conduct from that moment on, and he may even be satisfied with the fulfillment of the injunction imposed on him, including as a means of avoiding greater financial losses.

> It is unacceptable for the opposition to proceeding to be expressed in the form of an amendment to the initial application (art. 303, § 1, I, CPC). This is because the time limit for the amendment - at least 15 days - can coincide with, or even exceed, the time limit for appeals (art. 1.003, §2 with art. 231, CPC). Thus, if the plaintiff's statement were allowed within the time limit for an amendment, this could harm the defendant who, trusting in the possibility of stabilization, would stop appealing.[55]

For this reason, if there is no express request to continue the action, if the preliminary injunction is granted and is not challenged by the defendant, the case should be dismissed without judgment on the merits.

3.2.2 Decision granting preliminary injunctive relief

Although the assertion is obvious, in order for the phenomenon of stabilization to occur, a satisfactory injunction must exist

[54] DIDIER JR, Fredie; BRAGA, Paula Sarno; OLIVEIRA, Rafael Alexandria de. **Course on Civil Procedure**. 10 ed., Bahia: Editora Jus PODIVM, 2015, v. 2, p. 606.

positive decision in favor of the plaintiff, and any negative decision would not be suitable for stabilization.

With this in mind, the possibility of stabilizing injunctive relief in favor of the defendant is rejected, not only because articles 303 and 304 of the CPC expressly refer to the plaintiff, but for the simple fact that the defendant can only request injunctive relief against the plaintiff in an incidental manner and never antecedently, for obvious reasons.

3.2.3 Means of challenging the decision to grant preliminary injunctive relief

Although art. 304 of the CPC only mentions an appeal as an appropriate means of challenging the decision granting antecedent satisfactory relief, in order not to generate the effect of stabilization, the doctrine has admitted other means of defense or challenge other than that provided for by law.

In the literal expression of the law, only the interlocutory appeal filed by the defendant would be able to halt the stabilization process sought by the plaintiff, but there are other procedural mechanisms available to the defendant that produce the same practical effect, provided they are filed within the same appeal period.

Simply filing an interlocutory appeal in good time is enough to prevent the injunction from stabilizing, even if it is not subsequently heard.[56]

The logic put forward by the legislator was to invert the procedural onus, i.e. instead of the plaintiff having to bring the main action - if this is not in their interest - it will be up to the defendant to appeal the decision in order to avoid its crystallization through stabilization.

---

[56] SICA, Heitor Vitor Mendonga. **Twelve problems and eleven solutions to the so-called "stabilization of advance injunctions"**. Revista do Ministerio Publico do Rio de Janeiro n° 55, jan./mar. 2015, p. 94-95.

As has already been said, the doctrine has also opened up the possibility of the decision for advance satisfactory relief not being stabilized when the defendant seeks to challenge the decision within the time limit for presenting the appropriate appeal, whether by means of a request for a stay of proceedings, a complaint, a request for reconsideration or a defense presented in advance, as these would also be appropriate means of challenging the hasty judicial decision.

> Of course, it may happen that the defendant doesn't file an interlocutory appeal, but offers a response within the same time limit - or even expresses his opposition within the same time limit to the conciliation or mediation hearing. In this situation, it must be understood that the defendant's manifestation at the first level of jurisdiction serves just as well as the filing of an appeal to avoid the stabilization of the effects of the injunction. This solution has the advantage of saving the use of an interlocutory appeal and giving due importance to the expression of will contained in the response or the intention to attend the hearing. In both manifestations, the defendant's will is unequivocal in the sense of exhausting the debate by continuing the procedure.[57]

There is also a more radical position supported by Eduardo Talamini, who believes that it is necessary for the stabilization of advance satisfactory relief for the defendant to be in default[58] , i.e. for him not to present a defense, however, default is not one of the main reasons for this. assumptions for the application of art. 304 of the CPC.

Therefore, presenting a defense within the appeal period is a very important factor in avoiding stabilization, but the defendant's inertia, which depends on the occurrence of stabilization, does not require the occurrence of default.

---

[57] MARINONI, Luiz Guilherme; ARENHART, Sergio Cruz; MITIDIERO, Daniel. **Civil Procedure Course**. Sao Paulo: RT, 2015, vol. 2, p. 216.

[58] TALAMINI, Eduardo. **Guardianship of urgency in the Project for a new Civil Procedure Code:** the stabilization of the urgent measure and the 'monitoring' of the Brazilian process. Revista de Processo. Sao Paulo: RT, 2012, no. 209, p. 29.

3.2.4 An action for annulment as a means of not stabilizing or confirming a provisional advance injunction

As provided for in article 304, §§ 2 and 5 of the CPC, either party may bring an independent action for the purpose of reviewing, reforming or invalidating the preliminary injunction. This action will generally come from the defendant who has experienced the negative effects of the stabilized decision, but it may also come from the plaintiff who wishes to review it in order to improve his situation or even with the aim of seeking the effects of res judicata on the preliminary injunction that has been stabilized.

This new legal regime for emergency injunctions also brings with it the reversal of the procedural onus, since in the previous Code it was up to the plaintiff to bring the main action within the time limit set by law, under penalty of revocation of the injunction granted and termination of the case without judgment on the merits. Now, once the preliminary injunction has been obtained, if the plaintiff is satisfied, it will be up to the defendant to seek reversal of the injunction through the appropriate action, if he has not obtained it through the appropriate appeal procedure or other means of challenge.

Pursuant to article 304, paragraph 4 of the CPC, the judge who conducted the original proceedings will be competent to hear the main action, even establishing prevención.

In order to file the main action, the party must request that the action in which the anticipatory measure was granted be unsealed, and if it is a physical file (paper), a copy must be made to attach to the main action. Even if the main action is brought, the preliminary injunction will continue to have effects, because it has been stabilized; however, only an eventual meritorious decision can cause its effects to cease (art. 304, § 3, CPC).

There is concern and doubt among civil proceduralists about the impact that could be caused by filing an autonomous action to challenge an advance measure that has already been stabilized. It is clear that if the advance measure were to be weakened by the filing of a separate action, it would lose the meaning of the institute created, and could even generate an endless stream of injunctions that would follow one another.

> I don't think that the mere filing of the lawsuit could, in itself, have an impact on the execution (otherwise the already meager usefulness of the institute in question would be completely emptied). The defendant in the first case would have the burden of convincing the judge, in summary cognizance, to grant a preliminary injunction in order to suspend enforcement of the stabilized decision. The curious thing is that this second anticipatory decision (issued in the challenge) could also, provided the requirements outlined above are met, be stabilized. In this respect, I cannot refrain from raising the argument *ad terrorem* that the application of the stabilization technique in the claim brought on the basis of art. 304, §5, could be repeated *ad infinitum*... After a stabilization, the affected party could come to court and obtain a preliminary injunction which, in turn, would be stabilized, repeating the cycle indefinitely.[59]

In view of this, we can only wait for the court decisions that will follow and whether the positive effects envisioned by the legislator will be present in the practical world.

3.3. PARTIAL STABILIZATION OF PROVISIONAL INJUNCTIONS

Another point that has been the subject of much debate in the legal profession is whether or not it is possible to partially stabilize the advance provisional injunction. For some scholars, the mere fact that the defendant has appealed would prevent the aforementioned effect from being obtained.

On the other hand, some argue that there can be partial stabilization of the preliminary injunction when the defendant challenges only part of it, in other words, if there are cumulative claims and the judge grants them to the plaintiff, but there is only a partial appeal against them, they would have the effect of partially stabilizing the injunction.

> [...] or in the event that the plaintiff makes two requests, in simple cumulation, and the judge grants only one (e.g.: the victim of a non-

[59] SICA, Heitor Vitor Mendonga. **Twelve problems and eleven solutions to the so-called "stabilization of advance injunctions"**. Revista do Ministerio Publico do Rio de Janeiro n° 55, jan./mar. 2015, p. 95.

contractual tort requests an injunction to pay for urgent medical treatment and a monthly pension, but the judge grants an injunction for only the second measure). Considering that the projected system expands the possibilities for breaking up the subject of litigation - especially by textually accepting the partial trial on the merits (art. 356) - there is no reason to refuse partial stabilization, with a reduction in the subject of litigation that will be submitted to a trial based on exhaustive cognition.[60]

The latter position seems more logical, since the defendant may be satisfied with part of the injunction granted, even intending to remain inert in order to achieve stabilization, but may not be satisfied with the second part of the decision, which is harmful to him.

3.4. NEGOTIATED STABILIZATION

Although art. 304 of the CPC does not mention anything about the possibility of negotiating whether or not to stabilize the provisional guardianship, the parties may enter into an agreement before or during the court proceedings, within the limits of the general negotiation clause between the parties provided for in art. 190 of the CPC, in order to expand the general rule.

This possibility is so admissible that the Permanent Forum of Civil Proceduralists issued statement no. 32, which reads: "In addition to the hypothesis provided for in art. 304, it is possible to expressly negotiate the stabilization of antecedent satisfactory advance injunctive relief".

> For example, the parties can insert a clause in the articles of association to the effect that any preliminary injunctions in cases arising from the terms of that agreement, if granted, may: i) be stabilized regardless of the plaintiff's express request in the initial petition to that effect; ii) it being admitted that, in the face of the defendant's default and total inertia, the plaintiff has preserved the right to ask for the same.

---

[60] SICA, Heitor Vitor Mendonga. **Twelve problems and eleven solutions regarding the so-called "stabilization of advance injunctions"**. Revista do Ministerio Publico do Rio de Janeiro n° 55, jan./mar. 2015, p. 95.

> continuation of the process in order to obtain a decision with exhaustive cognition and the force of res judicata.[61]

Negotiated stabilization can generate greater solidity in legal business and confidence that litigation will be shortened by the pronouncement of the Judiciary in a summary judgment, and there is no reason why it should not be allowed in contemporary law, as can be seen from the position cited above.

3.5. CONSTITUTIONALITY OF STABILIZATION

As can be seen from this study, the current CPC has allowed for the autonomization and stabilization of summary injunctions, in other words, it has allowed a satisfactory emergency injunction granted in advance to survive and perpetuate its effects even if there is no main action, without the plaintiff having to request a definitive injunction, since the CPC only requires its mention in the initial application.

This guardianship, which has taken on a life of its own in the current CPC, resembles res judicata in its external effects, but conceptually departs from it, making it impossible to say that provisional satisfactory guardianship granted in advance can become res judicata, since it has not gone through the process of exhaustive cognition (full defense and adversarial proceedings).

It is at this point that some doctrinal controversy arises about this new procedural institute, especially about its autonomy and constitutionality.

There is strong support for the thesis that the stabilization technique provided for in satisfactory injunctive relief meets the desires of the court, in view of the crisis of material law, in the sense of the

[61] DIDIER JR, Fredie; BRAGA, Paula Sarno; OLIVEIRA, Rafael Alexandria de. **Course on Civil Procedure**. 10 ed., Bahia: Editora Jus PODIVM, 2015, v. 2, p. 611.

delay and even the unfeasibility of the definitive protection provided at the end of the process.

As the most varied civil procedure manuals state, the stabilization of satisfactory injunctive relief does not become res judicata and can be challenged by means of a proper appeal, which would prevent the definitive stabilization of the preliminary injunction.

However, there is a two (2) year time limit for bringing an action against the court, counting from the date of the action that extinguishes the satisfactory injunction granted in advance. It is precisely on this point that some scholars differ, as some believe that there is an unconstitutionality due to the permanent effects of unappealed injunctive relief, a force that would only come from res judicata obtained in a process in which there is exhaustive cognition.

MARINONI rejects the possibility of comparing the stabilization of satisfactory injunctions with res judicata, but admits that their effects are similar, which is why he criticizes and questions the novelty of the procedure:

> There is therefore nothing to prevent the legislator from designing differentiated procedures that are summary from a formal point of view (shortening the procedure) and from a material point of view (with summary cognition, limited to the probability of the right). What is of doubtful constitutional legitimacy is to *equate the effects of* the common procedure - carried out in an adversarial manner, with ample defense and the right to evidence - with the effects of a procedure whose formal and material brevity is extremely accentuated.[62]

On the other hand, there is plenty of doctrine supporting the constitutionality of the new procedural mechanism in the current CPC:

> The Code, on the other hand, leaves the door open for a later filing of the main action, of full cognition, to re-discuss the material right that is the object of the relief issued in the precedent process - reviewing, reforming or invalidating the satisfactory relief -, as can be seen from art. 304, § 2. However, even with the filing of the main action, the measure granted in the precedent procedure maintains its effects, as long as it is not reviewed, reformed or invalidated by the judge (art. 304, § 3). This twofold possibility, of the continuation of the provisional measure or subsequent improvement

---

[62] MARINONI, Luiz Guilherme; ARENHART, Sergio Cruz; MITIDIERO, Daniel. **Civil Procedure Course**. Sao Paulo: RT, 2015, vol. 2, p. 217.

of the merits process of full cognition, rules out, as the Italian doctrine points out, any consideration of the unconstitutionality of provisional protection, which would be based on the violation of the guarantee of defense or access to jurisdiction.[63]

Following this line of thought, MARINONI envisages the possibility of attacking the stabilized satisfactory injunction after the expiry of the period provided for in art. 304,

§ Paragraph 5 of the CPC:

> The blocking effect of the fundamental right to a fair trial, therefore, prevents the formation of res judicata in the case of preliminary injunctions requested in advance from being constitutional if the legal time limit has elapsed without exhausting cognition. This means that the stabilization of preliminary injunctions cannot achieve the authority of res judicata - which is peculiar to exhaustive cognition procedures. Once the two-year period has elapsed, it is still possible for cognition to be exhausted until the time limits laid down in substantive law for the stabilization of legal situations act on the legal sphere of the parties (for example, prescription, decay and suppression).[64]

The above position deserves respect, but does not stand up to a systematic analysis, since it is common in Brazilian law for decadence periods to be created by means of material or procedural law, as can be seen from the typical example of the rescission action provided for in article 975 of the CPC.

> **4.9. Does Stabilization apply to Rescission Actions?**
> I also don't see any other possible answer than *no.* In order to justify this assertion, it is almost idle to point out, at the outset, that the rescission action admits provisional relief, in order to halt the effectiveness of the rescinded decision, whether in the current system (art. 48943) or in the projected system (art. 969). However, the rescission action will not allow the plaintiff to opt for the application of the system provided for in arts. 303 and 304, because res judicata - which ultimately has a constitutional basis (art. 5, XXXVI) - could not give way in the face of a decision based on summary cognition. It's as simple as that.[65]

As we can see, the possibility of using the rescission action as a means of reversing the stabilization of the satisfactory guardianship is to be rejected, especially those who compare the procedural novelty to the

---

[63] THEODORO JR., Humberto. **Civil Procedure Course**. 56 ed. Rio de Janeiro: Forense, 2016, vol. 1, p. 675.
[64] MARINONI, Luiz Guilherme; ARENHART, Sergio Cruz; MITIDIERO, Daniel. **Civil Procedure Course**. Sao Paulo: RT, 2015, vol. 2, p. 218.
[65] SICA, Heitor Vitor Mendonqa. **Twelve problems and eleven solutions regarding the so-called "stabilization of advance injunctions"**. Revista do Ministerio Publico do Rio de Janeiro n° 55, jan./mar. 2015, p. 98.

monitoring action, against which there is the possibility of using the rescission action, whose situation has already been the subject of statement no. 33 of the Permanent Forum of Civil Proceduralists.[66]

3.6. STABILIZATION *VERSUS RES* JUDICATA (SIMILARITIES AND DISSIMILARITIES)

In order to draw comparisons or dissimilarities between the stabilization of interim relief and res judicata, it is crucial to make it clear that effectiveness is not to be confused with immutability, according to LIEBMAN[67] , since a decision can produce its effects regardless of whether it has become immune to subsequent alterations.

> The immutability of res judicata - an exceptional quality within the framework of the public function - cannot be attributed indiscriminately to any judicial act. What makes an act immune from review is not only the fact that it was preceded by an opportunity for the parties to express their views, but above all the depth of the cognition that can be developed.[68]

In the same way that effectiveness should not be confused with stability, since the antecedent satisfactory provisional protection, even before it stabilizes, already has full effectiveness to be executed, it happens, that in this case the execution must be provisional, while the provisional protection already stabilized by the effects of time (inertia of the defendant) gives rise to definitive execution.

There is also no escaping the comparison between immunity and stability, as these are different procedural phenomena, the former being typical only of res judicata.

---

[66] Statement no. 33 of the Permanent Forum of Civil Proceduralists: "There is no room for rescission in cases of stabilization of emergency injunctive relief".

[67] Efficacy and authority of the judgment and other writings on res judicata (with additions relating to Brazilian law). Translated by Alfredo Buzaid and Benvindo Aires. Translation of texts subsequent to the 1945 edition and notes on current Brazilian law by Ada Pellegrini Grinover. Rio de Janeiro: Forense, 1984, *passim.*

[68] TALAMINI, Eduardo. **Guardianship of urgency in the Project for a new Civil Procedure Code:** the stabilization of the urgent measure and the 'monitoring' of the Brazilian process. Revista de Processo. Sao Paulo: RT, 2012, no. 209, p. 28.

It is worth remembering that in the preliminary draft of the CPC by Ada Pellegrini Grinover[69] , provisional injunctions were given the status of res judicata after they were not challenged by the defendant within the time limit set.

The current CPC uses the term "stable", without ever talking about immutability, much less res judicata, as it did not intend to create or equate the new procedural institute with res judicata, having repelled such a claim in the reform proposal previously presented by Ada Pellegrini Grinover.

It is clear from the legislation in force that stabilized provisional protection is fully effective regardless of whether it is subsequently confirmed by a meritorious decision through a judge of exhaustive cognizance, which becomes optional, depending on the will of the parties to make or not make a material res judicata; or just settle for the stabilization of the right sought and granted in limine, avoiding all the natural wear and tear of the procedural clash and the corrosive effects of time.

The doctrinal position reproduced below, which technically demonstrates within the CPC itself the impossibility of comparing the stability of interim relief with res judicata, is enlightening:

> Even so, I believe that there is no res judicata. In order to reach this conclusion, I note, firstly, that §1 of art. 304 states that the stabilization of the provisional injunction takes place after the "termination of the proceedings", without stating whether *with* or *without a* decision on the merits. Art. 487 (which basically reproduces the hypotheses of art. 269 of the current CPC) does not include this hypothesis, while art. 485 (equivalent to the current art. 267) could cover the situation in its item X (which makes the provision merely exemplary by including in it the "other cases prescribed in this Code"). Thus, it is easier to fit this situation into the cases of terminating judgments, which would rule out art. 502 (which reserves the formation of res judicata for judgments on the merits).[70]

[69] The preliminary draft drawn up by Ada Pellegrini Grinover in 1997 proposed adding an eighth paragraph to art. 273 of the current CPC, which would read as follows: "If there is a challenge, the case will continue until final judgment. If there is no challenge, or if it is deemed inadmissible by the judge, the anticipatory provision will become a judgment on the merits, subject to appeal if it has suspensive effect, the defendant being exempt from costs and attorney's fees if he does not appeal. (Proposal to amend the Civil Procedure Code - Justification. Revista de processo, n. 86, p.191).

[70] SICA, Heitor Vitor Mendonga. **Twelve problems and eleven solutions to the so-called "stabilization of advance injunctions"**. Revista do Ministerio Publico do Rio de Janeiro n° 55, jan./mar. 2015, p. 93.

He goes on to say that res judicata, unlike the phenomenon of the stabilization of interim relief, has a double effect (negative and positive), while the latter only has a negative effect:

> Secondly, it must be recognized that res judicata has not only a negative function (which prevents the same dispute from being litigated again, as stated in art. 304, §5), but also a positive function (i.e. the decision must be observed in future cases between the same parties). The stabilized decision does not seem to have this positive function. After two years of the decision extinguishing the case, there is a *qualified stability* because, although it cannot be altered, it cannot be confused with *immunity* due to the lack of a positive function. Furthermore, it seems more appropriate to recognize that the explanation for this phenomenon rests on the institute of "decadence" (as occurs when it comes to the rescission action, *ex vi art.* 495 of the current CPC and art. 975 of the new **CPC33**), so that the extemporaneity of the demand made on the basis of art. 304, §2, would lead to the extinguishment of the case on the basis of art. 487, II.[71]

Although it is very clear that the stabilization of the satisfactory injunction granted in advance does not become res judicata, there are doctrines defending that, after this two-year period, material res judicata would be formed on the stabilized provisional decision.[72]

For those who argue that there is a similarity between stabilization and res judicata, it would be possible to file a rescission action after the two years that the parties had to file a challenge (art. 304, § 5, CPC) and did not do so.[73]

In the view of those who support this line of reasoning and equate the stabilization of injunctive relief with res judicata, as soon as the time limit for challenging the decision has elapsed, the time limit for filing a rescission action (art. 975, CPC) would automatically begin, and would also be characterized by a smaller scope for challenging the decision, now limited to the items in art. 966, CPC.

---

[71] *Ibid.,* 2015, p. 94.

[72] GRECO, Leonardo. Guardianship of **urgency and guardianship of evidence in the 2015 civil procedure code.** Revista Eletronica de Direito Processual - REDP, , 2014, vol 14, n. 1; MACEDO, Lucas Buril de; PEIXOTO, Ravi; FREIRE, Alexandre. **Selected Doctrine: Special Procedures, Provisional Guardianship and Transitional Law**. Salvador: Juspodivm, 2015, v. 4, p. 206.

[73] GAJARDONI, Fernando da Fonseca; DELLORE, Luiz; ROQUE, Andre Vasconcelos; OLIVEIRA JR., Zulmar Duarte de. **Teoria geral do processo - comentarios ao CPC de 2015 - parte geral**. Sao Paulo: Metodo, 2015, p. 903; REDONDO, Bruno Garcia. **Stabilization, modification and negotiation of preliminary injunctions: main controversies**. Revista de Processo. Sao Paulo: RT, vol. 244, jun. 2015, p. 187-188.

According to this doctrinal current, the existence of res judicata would be based on the removal of the relationship between res judicata and exaurient cognition, which would not be suitable for the current Codex. Since res judicata would only be the phenomenon that prevents the (re)filing of lawsuits aimed at modifying a previous judgment on the merits, it could be included in the situation of provisional protection that has not been challenged within two years.

They go on to say that §6 of art. 304 would not prevent this conclusion, since it would only deal with the non-existence of res judicata of the stabilized decision, but not with the legal situation that would come into existence after the two years.[74]

This is also the conclusion of other authors, given that there would be a supposed merit to this procedure of preliminary injunction (danger of damage or risk to the useful outcome of the process and the probability of the right) and also the fact that exhaustive cognition would not be an obstacle to attributing the quality of res judicata to this decision, since any historical judgment would only be of verisimilitude and the only difference between this decision and a judgment in the ordinary procedure would be the contradiction, which would have been understood as dispensable by the defendant.[75]

> Contrary to what Bruno Garcia Redondo argues, §6 of art. 304 seems to completely prohibit the existence of res judicata. There is no indication that this stabilization could be transformed into res judicata after the two years of the review action have passed. The discussion, in fact, should not go beyond the (in)existence of exhaustive cognition, since nothing would prevent the legislator from imposing the production of res judicata in this procedure. A similar situation occurs in the monitoring action, in which even a guardianship of evidence - also of provisional cognition - has the capacity, if not challenged, to be covered by res judicata (art. 701, CPC/2015). The obstacle to this new procedure is legislative, and it is not up to doctrine to change the nature of stabilization to res judicata. It is an attempt to fill an

[74] REDONDO, Bruno Garcia. **Stabilization, modification and negotiation of preliminary injunctions:** main controversies. Revista de Processo. Sao Paulo: RT, v. 244, jun. 2015, p. 187-188.

[75] GOMES, Frederico Augusto; RUDINIKI NETO, Rogerio. **Stabilization of injunctive relief:** some controversial issues. MACEDO, Lucas Buril de; PEIXOTO, Ravi; FREIRE, Alexandre. **Selected Doctrine: Special Procedures, Provisional Guardianship and Transitional Law**. Salvador: Juspodivm, 2015, vol. 4, p. 170.

axiological gap[76] illegitimately and should be rejected.[77]

Although I respect the above position, I cannot agree with it, since it is based on probability, it does not mean that the protection becomes immutable, but only *stable,* so that the party harmed by the measure (any of them) can, if it is in their interest, reopen it (since the absence of an appeal extinguishes the process) in order to prove, in a more in-depth way, the non-existence or unfoundedness of the stabilized claim.

Because of the double application of paragraph 2 of Article 304 of the new CPC in favor of the plaintiff or the defendant, giving them the possibility of suing the other in order to review, reform or invalidate the stabilized protection.

On the other hand, if the interested party doesn't file the main action within the time limit set by the CPC (two years) - counted from the date of notification of the termination of the proceedings - then the stabilized protection will become definitive, *and* nothing more can be done in this regard, much less the filing of a rescission action as the authors cited above maintain.

> The legislator states that the decision granting the preliminary injunction will not become res judicata (it will only be stable), but its effects cannot be removed in any way if, after two years, an action has not been brought to exhaust the cognition.[78]

MARINONI wonders how to qualify the strength of the provisional guardianship stabilized after the passage of time without the proposition of an exhaustive appeal, since the legislator did not make it clear in the Code, but

---

[76] The axiological lacuna consists of a regulation of a given factual support in a way that is not satisfactory to the interpreter. There is not really a lacuna, but a disagreement in the valuation of the way in which the subject has been treated normatively. (GUASTINI, Riccardo. **Problemas de conocimiento del derecho vigente**. MORATONES, Carles Cruz; BLANCO, Carolina Fernandez; BELTRAN, Jordi Ferrer (ed). **Legal security and democracy in Ibero-America**. Madrid: Marcial Pons, 2015, p. 24), *apud* COSTA, Eduardo Jose da Fonseca. **Stabilization and the immutability of anticipated effects.** http://justificando.com/2015/10/16/a-estabilizacao-e-a- imutabilidade-das-eficacias-antecipadas/, viewed on 24/11/2016.

[77] COSTA, Eduardo Jose da Fonseca. **The stabilization and immutability of anticipated efficacies.** http://justificando.com/2015/10/16/a-estabilizacao-e-a-imutabilidade-das-eficacias-antecipadas/, viewed on 24/11/2016.

[78] MARINONI, Luiz Guilherme; ARENHART, Sergio Cruz; MITIDIERO, Daniel. **Civil Procedure Course**. Sao Paulo: RT, 2015, vol. 2, p. 216.

left the obvious path for interpretation, since in the absence of an exhaustive appeal the decision will become "unassailable", in other words: "immutable" and "indisputable".[79]

Some claim that this is a novelty in our current CPC, but they are wrong, as this procedural model is already known through the monitoring action, the defendant's default, confissao ficta, etc. The CPC has only established a general rule, recognizing that provisional protection can become stable and definitive.

What's more, there's no way of questioning the legality of the procedure or any possible unconstitutionality in the face of the possibility of stabilizing the provisional guardianship without an exhaustive hearing, as this was the option chosen by the legislator to make the process more effective and generate practical effects for the parties, since time has proven to be very cruel and corrosive to the claims of the contenders.

Another point that still generates controversy is the form of enforcement of the stabilized provisional guardianship, with some arguing that enforcement would be provisional due to the absence of an exhaustive judgment, however, there is no way to admit the provisionality of an enforcement whose decision is no longer subject to review, since it is stabilized by the effects of time, not along the lines of res judicata, but with its own characteristics provided for in art. 304 of the CPC.

Having said that, it is clear that although the practical effects of res judicata and the stabilization of interim relief are similar, conceptually there is no way of comparing them, simply because one originates from an exhaustive judgment and the other from a summary judgment; however, it can never be denied at first sight that both are immutable and indisputable, provided that the respective requirements laid down in the CPC are complied with.

Finally, I would like to borrow a link from Calmon de Passos in the

[79] *Ibid.,* 2015, p. 217.

1980s about the precautionary process, which generated some controversy among proceduralists, and which I have adapted to the current Civil Procedure Code:

> I dare say, and forgive me for being so bold, that decisions on the merits, in a precautionary action, are not subject to modification if there has been no change in the factual situation - the situation of danger - that led to the decision, or if there has been no change in the situation of law in terms of the plausibility of the protection favorable to the plaintiff. Only a change in one of these constituent elements of the cause of action authorizes the modification. And if the measure is rejected, only a new situation of danger, or changes in the conditions previously indicated as the basis for the request, or a request for a different measure from the previous one, can legitimize the request for a new precautionary measure. This immutability may not be called res judicata, but it is immutable. What should we call it if we don't want to place it in the noble family of contentious jurisdiction proceedings? Is it a problem of preference? Hermengarde, Febroniana, Ocridalina or something similar. But she is a woman like the other. Or to be more specific: the immutability of the decision with repercussions outside the precautionary process is. And so we have said.[80]

Lastly, comparing res judicata and the stabilization of provisional injunctions is undue, from the conceptual point of view of both.

the techniques, but it is no exaggeration to say that both have certain practical similarities once the two-year period has elapsed, counting from the date on which the defendant was informed of the extinguishment of the action that made the provisional protection possible, since the stabilization becomes immutable and indisputable, only not reaching the immunity that is a special characteristic of res judicata.

---

[80] PASSOS, Jose Joaquim Calmon de. **Comentarios ao Codigo** de **Processo Civil**. Sao Paulo: RT, 1984, vol. 10, p. 237.

4 FINAL CONSIDERATIONS

After concluding this study, which was divided into three essential phases, the first dealt with res judicata, the second with interim relief and the last aimed to delve deeper into the phenomenon of stabilization of satisfactory interim relief granted in advance.

It has become clear that, technically, res judicata can never be compared to the stabilization of interim relief, even if at certain times it can be admitted that in practice they are similar after a certain period of time.

On the other hand, it is well known that the legal certainty of res judicata is much greater than the stabilization of interim relief, even if it is no longer possible to use any means of appeal against it or even if the time limit for bringing an action to challenge it, as provided for in art. 304, § 5 of the CPC, has expired.

In this vein, it has been shown that although the phenomenon of stabilization of provisional injunctions has already been experienced in our law through the monitoring action, there is no way to accept the minority opinion of those who preach that it would be possible to file a rescission action after the time limit for filing an opposition action has expired (art. 304, § 5 of the CPC), and the issue has even been analyzed by the members of the Permanent Forum of Civil Proceduralists, meriting the issuance of Statement No. 33.

What's more, the mechanisms for controlling res judicata are infinitely inferior to the means of challenge that can lead to the destabilization of satisfactory interim relief granted in advance, since it would be enough for the defendant to file the appropriate appeal (interlocutory appeal) or another effective means of opposing the court decision and it would never stabilize, even if its effects continue to endure over time, given the possibility of the appeal not being upheld, but as has been said, this is enough to curb the phenomenon of stabilization.

Failure to grant an appeal or to overturn the preliminary injunction by another appropriate procedural means will not prevent the phenomenon of stabilization from being halted, since the legislator did not set the reversal of the decision as a requirement for preventing stabilization, but only that it be contested in some way, and some scholars even support the possibility of an appeal by means other than an appeal.

There is also no denying that the defendant's lack of interest or inertia will have very solid effects on the preliminary injunction that grants provisional protection in advance, since stabilization will allow the right granted provisionally to be definitively enforced, even if a challenge is filed within two years.

The plaintiff's situation may be even better once the two-year period has elapsed, counting from the date of the decision that extinguished the action granting provisional protection, because it will no longer be up to the defendant to challenge that stabilized decision, since it has also acquired the status of immutable and indisputable, however, even though it has acquired these characteristics of res judicata, it cannot be equated with it, however strange it may seem at first.

Although some scholars insist on linking the institutes of res judicata and the effects of stabilization to interim relief, there is no denying that certain practical effects are indeed identical (immutability and indisputability), except for the *way* in which they operate, making the technical distinction (dissimilarity) between them very clear.

Therefore, even if we conclude that both res judicata and the stabilization of interim relief are permeated by immutability and indisputability, we cannot reach the same conclusion when we talk about immunity, because stabilization only affects res judicata in terms of its negative effects, whereas immunity is a positive effect that is only characteristic of res judicata.

To say that the stabilization of satisfactory interim relief granted in advance is identical to res judicata is a gross error, given that the former comes from a summary judgment and is perfected (stabilized) over time in the face of the defendant's inertia, while the latter is only obtained through an exhaustive judgment, guaranteeing the parties the right to a full defense and adversarial proceedings.

It is also perceptible and permissible to conclude that the introduction of the institute of stabilization of provisional protection will bring greater effectiveness to judicial protection, as well as a reduction in the number of cases pending before the Judiciary, in view of cognitive and procedural summarization, as long as they are correctly handled by the operators of the law and correctly interpreted by the Judiciary, under penalty of trivializing the phenomenon of stabilization and practical ineffectiveness, as already preached by a few scholars who do not believe in the power of the new technique inaugurated.

In this way, the application of this new procedural technique can, in certain cases, produce immediate satisfaction of the interests of the plaintiff and often of the defendant himself, who does not want to extend the legal dispute, since the parties would be satisfied or would not see the possibility of overturning the decision through appeals, as well as lowering the cost of procedural costs and attorney's fees.

Furthermore, because the technique of stabilizing provisional injunctions is new in our Civil Procedure Law, despite its clear origins in the monitoring procedure already used in Portuguese law, there are clear doctrinal disagreements about the new institute, from its constitutionality to comparisons or dissimilarities with res judicata, however, the majority of those who believe in the promising future of the stabilization of interim relief and its inclusion in the new CPC, inspired by foreign law (Italy and France), should be right.

We can only wait for the national courts to take a stand on the still controversial issues surrounding provisional injunctions, especially the stabilization technique, in order to ensure that this new procedural institute can have positive effects on the resolution of legal disputes and shorten the procedural lifespan and the satisfaction of the parties at the end of the case.

REFERENCES

ARAGAO, Egas Dirceu. **Sentence and res judicata**. Rio de Janeiro: AIDE, 1992.

ASSIS, Araken de. **Cumulapao** de **apoes**. 4 ed. Sao Paulo: RT, 2002.

BAPTISTA DA SILVA, Ovidio. **Precautionary Process**. 3 ed. Rio de Janeiro: Forense, 2006.

BODART, Bruno Vinicius de Ros. **Guardianship of Evidence**. Sao Paulo: RT, 2014.

CABRAL, Antonio do Passo. **Coisa julgada e preclusoes dinamicas**. 2 ed. Salvador: Editora Jus Podivm, 2014.

COSTA, Eduardo Jose da Fonseca. Stabilization and the immutability of anticipated effects. http://iustificando.eom/2015/10/16/a-estabilizacao-e-a-imutabilidade-das-eficacias-antecipadas/, viewed on 24/11/2016.

COSTA, Eduardo Jose da Fonseca. **Precautionary sentence, cognition and res judicata** - reflections in honor of the memory of Ovidio Baptista. Revista de Processo. Sao Paulo: RT, 2011, no. 191, p. 368.

COSTA, Eduardo Jose da Fonseca. **Guardianship of evidence in the draft new CPC - an analysis of its presuppositions**. The future of Civil Procedure in Brazil - a critical analysis of the draft new CPC. Belo Horizonte: Forum, 2011, p. 171, note 8.

DIDIER JR, Fredie; BRAGA, Paula Sarno; OLIVEIRA, Rafael Alexandria de. **Civil Procedure Course**. 10 ed., Bahia: Editora Jus PODIVM, 2015, v. 2.

FUX, Luiz. Guardianship of **Security and Guardianship of Evidence**. Sao Paulo: Saraiva, 1996.

GAJARDONI, Fernando da Fonseca; DELLORE, Luiz; ROQUE, Andre Vasconcelos; OLIVEIRA JR., Zulmar Duarte de. **Teoria geral do processo -** comentarios ao CPC de 2015 - parte geral. Sao Paulo: Metodo, 2015.

GRECO, Leonardo. **Guardianship of urgency and guardianship of evidence in the 2015 civil procedure code.** Electronic Journal of Procedural Law - REDP, 2014, vol 14, n. 1.

MACEDO, Lucas Buril de; PEIXOTO, Ravi; FREIRE, Alexandre. **Selected Doctrine: Special Procedures, Provisional Guardianship and Transitional Law.** Salvador: Juspodivm, 2015, vol. 4.

MENESTRINA, Francesco. **La pregiudiciale nel processo civil.** p. 97, *apud* MARINONI; ARENHART e MITIDIERO, 2015.

MIRANDA NETO, Fernando Gama de. **A ponderagao de interesses na tutela de urgência irreversivel**. Rio de Janeiro: Lumen Juris, 2005.

MITIDIERO, Daniel. Res **judicata, objective limits and preclusive efficacy**. Introduction to the Study of Civil Procedure - first lines of an emerging paradigm. Porto Alegre: Fabris Editor, 2004.

MOREIRA, Jose Carlos Barbosa. **Preclusive efficacy of res judicata in the Brazilian civil procedure system**. Themes of Procedural Law. Sao Paulo:

Saraiva, 1977.

PASSOS, Jose Joaquim Calmon de. **Comentarios ao Codigo** de **Processo Civil**. Sao Paulo: RT, 1984, vol. 10.

PORTO, Sergio Gilberto. **Comments on the Civil Procedure Code**. Sao Paulo: RT, 2000, vol. 6.

REDONDO, Bruno Garcia. **Stabilization, modification and negotiation of preliminary injunctions: main controversies**. Revista de Processo. Sao Paulo: RT, vol. 244, June 2015.

SICA, Heitor Vitor Mendonpa. **Twelve problems and eleven solutions regarding the so-called "stabilization of advance injunctions"**. Revista do Ministerio Publico do Rio de Janeiro n° 55, jan./mar. 2015.

SILVA, Ovidio Baptista da. **Civil Procedure Course. Process of Knowledge**. 5 ed. Sao Paulo: RT, 2000, v. 1.

TALAMINI, Eduardo. Res **judicata and its revision**. Sao Paulo: RT, 2005.

TALAMINI, Eduardo. **The examination of Brazilian court judgments by the Inter-American Court of Human Rights**. In: Meios de Impugnapao ao julgado civil. Studies in Honor of Jose Carlos Barbosa Moreira. Adroaldo Furtado Fabricio (coord.). Rio de Janeiro: Forense, 2007.

TALAMINI, Eduardo. **Guardianship of urgency in the Project for a new Civil Procedure Code:** the stabilization of the urgent measure and the 'monitoring' of the Brazilian process. Revista de Processo. Sao Paulo: RT, 2012, n°. 209.

TALAMINI, Eduardo. **Tutela Monitoria**. 2 ed. Sao Paulo: RT, 2001.

TESHEINER, Jose Maria. **Efficacy of sentences and res judicata in civil proceedings**. Sao Paulo: RT, 2001.

THEODORO JR., Humberto. **Civil Procedure Course.** 56 ed. Rio de Janeiro: Forense, 2015, vol. 1.

THEODORO JR., Humberto. **Processo Cautelar**. 22 ed. Sao Paulo: Leud, 2005.

THEODORO JR., Humberto. **Anticipated Injunction - Evolution - Comparative View - Brazilian Law and European Law**. Scientific bases for a renewed procedural law. Sao Paulo: Instituto Brasileiro de Direito Processual Brasileiro vol.1, mai.- 2008.

YOSHIKAWA, Eduardo Henrique de Oliveira. **The expansion of the preclusive efficacy of res judicata in matters of competition law**: considerations regarding art. 98, § 4, of the new CADE Law (Law 12.529/2011). Revista de Processo. Sao Paulo: RT, 2013, no. 222.

ZAVASCKI, Teori Albino. **Antecipagao de Tutela**. 2 ed. Sao Paulo: Saraiva, 1999.

MIX
Papier aus verantwortungsvollen Quellen
Paper from responsible sources
FSC® C105338

Printed by Books on Demand GmbH, Norderstedt / Germany